# Welcome to
## Table Talk

**Table Talk** helps children and adults explore the Bible together. Each day provides a short family Bible time which, with your own adaptation, could work for ages 4 to 12. It includes optional follow–on material which takes the passage further for older children. There are also suggestions for linking **Table Talk** with **XTB** children's notes.

**Who can use Table Talk?**

### Table Talk

A short family Bible time for daily use. Table Talk takes about five minutes, maybe at breakfast, or after an evening meal. Choose whatever time and place suits you best as a family. Table Talk includes a simple discussion starter or activity that leads into a short Bible reading. This is followed by a few questions.

- **Families**
- **One adult with one child**
- **A teenager with a younger brother or sister**
- **Children's leaders with their groups**
- **Any other mix that works for you!**

### XTB

**XTB** children's notes help 7-11 year olds to get into the Bible for themselves. They are based on the same Bible passages as **Table Talk**. You will find suggestions for how **XTB** can be used alongside **Table Talk** on the next page.

In the next three pages you'll find suggestions for how to use Table Talk, along with hints and tips for adapting it to your own situation. If you've never done anything like this before, check out our web page for further help (go to www.thegoodbook.co.uk and click on Daily Reading) or write in for a fact sheet.

**THE SMALL PRINT**

Table Talk is published by The Good Book Company, 37 Elm Road, New Malden, Surrey, KT3 3HB
Tel: 0845 225 0880. www.thegoodbook.co.uk   email: alison@thegoodbook.co.uk   Written by Alison Mitchell.
Fab pictures by Kirsty McAllister. Bible quotations taken from the Good News Bible.
**AUSTRALIA:** Distributed by Matthias Media. Tel: (02) 9663 1478; email: info@matthiasmedia.com.au

# HOW TO USE
# Table Talk

**Table Talk** is designed to last for up to three month How you use it depends on what works for you. W have included 65 full days of material in this issue, plus some more low-key suggestions for another 2 days (at the back of the book). We would like to encourage you to work at establishing a pattern of family reading. The first two weeks are the hardest

**DAY 1**
**What shall we do?**

**KEYPOINT**
This is the main point you should be trying to convey. Don't read this out—it often gives away the end of the story!

**Table Talk** is based on the same Bible passages as *XTB*, but usually only asks for two or three verses to be read out loud. The full *XTB* passage is listed at the top of each **Table Talk** page. If you are using **Table Talk** with older children, read the full *XTB* passage rather than the shorter version.

The main part of **Table Talk** is designed to be suitable for younger children. *Building Up* includes more difficult questions designed for older children, or those with more Bible knowledge.

As far as possible, if your children are old enough to read the Bible verses for themselves, encourage them to find the answers in the passage and to tell you which verse the answer is in. This will help them to get used to handling the Bible for themselves.

The **Building Up** section is optional. It is designed to build on the passage studied in Table Talk (and XTB). Building Up includes some additional questions which reinforce the main teaching point, apply the teaching more directly, or follow up any difficult issues raised by the passage.

## Linking with *XTB*

The **XTB** children's notes are based on the same passages as **Table Talk**. There are a number of ways in which you can link the two together:
- Children do **XTB** on their own. Parents then follow these up later (see suggestions below).
- A child and adult work through **XTB** together.
- A family uses **Table Talk** together at breakfast. Older children then use **XTB** on their own later.
- You use **Table Talk** on its own, with no link to **XTB**.

## FOLLOWING UP XTB

If your child uses **XTB** on their own it can be helpful to ask them later to show you (or tell you) what they've done. Some useful starter questions are:

- Can you tell me what the reading was about?

- Is there anything you didn't understand or want to ask about?

- Did anything surprise you in the reading? Was there anything that would have surprised the people who first saw it or read about it?

- What did you learn about God, Jesus or the Holy Spirit?

- Is there anything you're going to do as a result of reading this passage?

Table Talk is deliberately not too ambitious. Most families find it quite hard to set up a regular pattern of reading the Bible together—and when they do meet, time is often short. So Table Talk is designed to be quick and easy to use, needing little in the way of extra materials, apart from pen and paper now and then.

## BUT!!

Most families have special times when they **can** be more ambitious, or do have some extra time available. Here are some suggestions for how you can use Table Talk as the basis for a special family adventure...

## PICNIC

Take Table Talk with you on a family picnic. Thank God for His beautiful Creation.

### WALK

Go for a walk together. Stop somewhere with a good view and read Genesis 1v1—2v4.

## GETTING TOGETHER

Invite another family for a meal, and to read the Bible together. The children could make a poster based on the passage.

## MUSEUM

Visit a museum to see a display from Bible times. Use it to remind yourselves that the Bible tells us about real people and real history.

## HOLIDAYS

Set aside a special time each day while on holiday. Choose some unusual places to read the Bible together—on the beach, up a mountain, in a boat... Take some photos to put on your Table Talk display when you get back from holiday.

You could try one of the special holiday editions of XTB and Table Talk—**Christmas Unpacked, Easter Unscrambled** and **Summer Signposts.**

# Have an adventure!

## FOOD!

Eat some food linked with the passage you are studying. For example Manna (biscuits made with honey, Exodus 16v31), Unleavened bread or Honeycomb (Matthew 3v4— but don't try the locusts!)

## DISPLAY AREA

We find it easier to remember and understand what we learn when we have something to look at. Make a Table Talk display area, for pictures, Bible verses and prayers. Add to it regularly.

## VIDEO

A wide range of Bible videos are available—from simple cartoon stories, to whole Gospels filmed with real life actors. (Your local Christian bookshop should have a range.) Choose one that ties in with the passages you are reading together. **_Note:_** Use the video **in addition** to the Bible passage, not **instead** of it!

## PRAYER DIARY

As a special project, make a family prayer diary. Use it to keep a note of things you pray for—and the answers God gives you. This can be a tremendous help to children (and parents!) to learn to trust God in prayer as we see how He answers over time.

Go on—try it!

## DRAMA OR PUPPETS

Take time to dramatise a Bible story. Maybe act it out (with costumes if possible) or make some simple puppets to retell the story.

**Enough of the introduction, let's get going...**

## TWO KINGDOMS:

God's people, the Israelites, had split into two kingdoms.

**1.** The <u>northern</u> kingdom was called **Israel**. Its capital city was **Samaria**.

**2.** The <u>southern</u> kingdom was called **Judah**. Its capital was **Jerusalem**.

*Find all of these places on the map.*

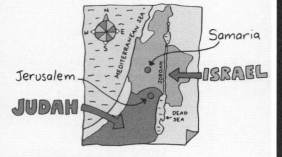

## TWO KINDS OF KING:

The kings of Israel and Judah came in two kinds:

**1.** Kings who <u>loved</u> God and obeyed His laws.

**2.** Kings who <u>turned away</u> from God and served pretend gods (statues) instead.

*We'll meet both kinds of king as we read the book of 2 Kings.*

## TWO PROPHETS:

In the books of 1 Kings and 2 Kings we meet two of God's prophets (messengers). They were called Elijah and Elisha. *Go back to the 'Read' section in today's Table Talk section to find out more about them...*

Elijah

Elisha

---

## DAY 1
# Two by two

**KEYPOINT**
God spoke to His people through His prophets. Today He speaks to us through the Bible.

Today's passages are:
**Table Talk**: 2 Kings 2v11
**XTB**: 2 Kings 2v11

**TABLE TALK**

Look round the room to see how many things you can spot that come in **pairs**, or have the number **2** on them.

There will be lots of **two**s today. Read **Notes for Parents** to find out why.

**READ**

*Two prophets:* God spoke to His people—and their kings—through His prophets (God's messengers). In the book of 1 Kings we can read about the fiery prophet **Elijah**. He spoke God's Word to the Israelites, telling them to turn away from pretend gods and turn back to God.

Amazingly, Elijah didn't die! God was so pleased with him, that He took Elijah up to heaven! Read the passage to find out how. **Read 2 Kings 2v11**

**TALK**

How did Elijah go to heaven? (v11) (*In a whirlwind, with a chariot of fire.*) Elijah's servant, called **Elisha**, took over as God's prophet. In the next few days we'll read about how God used Elisha to do amazing things.

**THINK**

**God spoke** to His people through His two prophets, Elijah and Elisha. Today, **God speaks** to His people (Christians) through His Word the Bible:

*Dear God, thank You for giving us Your Word, the Bible, so that we can know You better and better. Please help us to understand what we read, and to obey what You tell us. Amen*

**PRAY**

### Building up

Copy the prayer above onto some paper. Keep it in your Bible, and pray it each day before doing Table Talk.

# DAY 2
## Oodles of oil

**KEYPOINT**
God cares for those who no one else cares for. We can follow His example.

Today's passages are:
**Table Talk:** 2 Kings 4v1-7
**XTB:** 2 Kings 4v1-7

**TABLE TALK**

If you can, put some olive oil on the table. Ask your child if they know where it comes from and what it's used for.

Olive trees were among the most common trees of Israel. Farmers harvested the olives by shaking or beating the tree so that the fruit fell to the ground. The fruit was then crushed to produce oil.

**READ**

In today's reading, God used **Elisha** (His prophet) to help a lady who was in loads of trouble. Her husband had died, and she couldn't pay the money she owed. It looked as though she would lose both of her sons... **Read 2 Kings 4v1-7**

**TALK**

What did the woman have? (v2) (*A little olive oil.*) What did Elisha tell her to collect? (v3) (*Loads of jars.*) The widow only had a <u>little</u> oil. How many of the jars did she fill? (v6) (*All of them!*)

The woman <u>didn't</u> have enough oil, so how do you think all those jars became full? (*God turned her little bit of oil into oodles of oil!*)

**THINK**

God cares for those no one else cares for. <u>We</u> can follow His example. Think of some ways that <u>you</u> can care for those who need help. (*Eg: visiting an old lady who has no family, raising money for charity...*)

**PRAY**

Now ask God to help you to do this.

### Building up
*Tearfund* are a Christian charity who help out people without food, money or homes. You can find out about them from their website at www.tearfund.org

# DAY 3
## So-o-o kind

**KEYPOINT**
God is so-o-o kind to His people.

Today's passages are:
**Table Talk:** 2 Kings 4v8-17
**XTB:** 2 Kings 4v8-17

**TABLE TALK**

What do you like about your bedroom?

Elisha didn't have his own room, because he travelled so much. But that was about to change... **Read 2 Kings 4v8-10**

**TALK**

Yesterday we saw how God used Elisha to look after a widow and her sons. Now God used another woman to look after Elisha! What did she give Elisha every time he was in the area? (v8) (*A meal.*) Then what did she build for Elisha? (v10) (*A room of his own.*)

**Wow!** That was so-o-o kind! She showed her love for God by being kind to Elisha.

**READ**

Elisha wanted to do something for her as a thank you. **Read 2 Kings 4v11-17**

What did Elisha tell the woman? (v16) (*She would have a son in a year's time.*) The woman didn't want to get her hopes up. "Man of God, don't lie to me," she said. But Elisha was serious about thanking this woman, and he knew that God would give her a baby. Was he right? (v17) (*Yes, she had a son.*)

**PRAY**

**Wow!** God is so-o-o kind to His people. Think of some things <u>you</u> can thank God for—and then do it!

### Building up
This woman did a lot for Elisha. Think of someone who has done a lot for you. How will you thank them? (*A letter? A phone call? A visit? A present?...*)

# Dead or alive?

# Notes for Parents

> **KEYPOINT**
> God answered Elisha's prayers and brought the woman's son back to life.

Today's passages are:
**Table Talk:** 2 Kings 4v32-37
**XTB:** 2 Kings 4v18-37

 **TABLE TALK**

Remember the woman in yesterday's story? What did she do for Elisha? (*Gave him meals and built him a room.*) What did God give her and her husband? (*A baby boy.*)

But that's not the end of the story! Read the picture story in **Notes for Parents** to see what happened next.

 **READ**

Was <u>this</u> the end of the story? **Read 2 Kings 4v32-37** to find out.

 **TALK**

What was the first thing Elisha did when he reached the boy? (v33) (*He prayed.*) Then what did Elisha do? (v34-35) (*He laid down on the boy's body, twice.*) What did the boy do? (v35) (*He sneezed seven times and opened his eyes.*)

**Wow!** God answered Elisha's prayers and brought the boy back to life!

 **THINK**

We can talk to God about anything. <u>Nothing</u> is too hard for Him! He won't always answer our prayers in the way we expect—but He will always do what's right and good.

What do you want to talk to God about right now?

 **PRAY**

## Building up

Why do you think God allowed this boy to die? (*Clue: What did this show his mother—and us!—about God?*) God loves to give **life** in a hopeless situation. <u>We</u> are hopeless too, without Jesus. But if we have put our trust in Jesus, God gives us **eternal life**—so that we can know Him now, and one day live with Him in heaven.

Some years later, at harvest time, the boy went out one morning to join his father.

Suddenly, he cried out.

My head! My head!

Carry him to his mother.

The boy sat on his mother's lap until midday, and then he died.

She carried him up to Elisha's room, and put him on the bed.

Send a servant with a donkey.

I need to go to see Elisha.

She went as fast as she could to Mount Carmel, where Elisha was.

When Elisha heard her news, he spoke to his servant, Gehazi.

Hurry! Take my stick and go.

Go straight to the house and hold my stick over the boy.

Gehazi held Elisha's stick over the boy...

...but there was no sign of life.

Taken from 2 Kings 4v18-31.

# DAY 5
# Pot of... death!

**KEYPOINT**
Elisha wasn't special. Neither was the flour! It is <u>God</u> who is special.

Today's passages are:
**Table Talk:** 2 Kings 4v38-41
**XTB:** 2 Kings 4v38-41

**TABLE TALK**

Put a bag of flour on the table. What could you do with it?

**READ**

In today's story there's a famine in the land, which means there wasn't enough food. **Read 2 Kings 4v38-40**

**TALK**

What did Elisha tell his servant to do? (v38) (*Cook a big pot of stew*.) One of the men found a wild vine. What did he pick? (v39) (*Some gourds [fruit]*.) They cooked the gourds with the stew, but what happened when they tried to eat it? (v40) (*They found it was poisonous*.)

**READ**

It looked like they would have to throw the poisonous stew away—even though there was a famine. But Elisha had other ideas... **Read 2 Kings 4v41**

**THINK**

What did Elisha put in the stew? (v41) (*Flour*.) Flour (meal) is pretty ordinary. You can't do much with it except bake (or make flour bombs!). But after the flour was added, the poisonous stew was good to eat. Was this because the flour was special? Or because Elisha was special? Or because something or someone else was special?

**PRAY**

The special person in this story is God! It was **God** who used ordinary flour to make that stew safe. We can always talk to God about our problems. And He may well use something ordinary to sort things out for us. Talk to Him now.

## Building up
It would have been silly for those prophets to start worshipping a bag of flour instead of God! But Paul warns us to be careful to worship the Creator (God), <u>not</u> the things He created. **Read Romans 1v25**.

# DAY 6
# Signposts

**KEYPOINT**
Elisha's miracles showed he <u>spoke</u> for God. Jesus' miracles showed He <u>was</u> God.

Today's passages are:
**Table Talk:** 2 Kings 4v42-44
**XTB:** 2 Kings 4v42-44

**TABLE TALK**

Miracles are like **signposts**. Which three have we read about so far? (*1—The little bit of oil that turned into oodles of oil. 2—The dead boy who was brought back to life. 3—The poisonous stew that was made good to eat.*)

**READ**

These miracles all pointed to <u>who</u> Elisha was—He was God's messenger. It was <u>God's</u> power, but <u>Elisha</u> spoke for Him. Now for another miracle...
**Read 2 Kings 4v42-44**

**TALK**

There was a famine where Elisha was, so this man had brought food. How much did he bring? (v42) (*20 loaves of barley bread*.) How many hungry men were there? (v43) (*100 men*) The loaves of bread would have been small—nothing like enough to feed 100 men! But what had God said? (v43) (*"They will eat and have some left over."*) Did God's words come true? (v44) (*Yes!*)

**THINK**

Does that remind you of another story? Who else fed a hungry crowd with a tiny amount of food? (*Jesus*) Jesus fed a HUGE crowd (5000 men, plus women & children) with one boy's packed lunch!

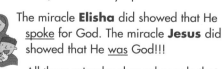

The miracle **Elisha** did showed that He <u>spoke</u> for God. The miracle **Jesus** did showed that He <u>was</u> God!!!

**PRAY**

All those miracles showed people that Elisha was God's messenger. So they should <u>listen</u> to him. And <u>we</u> should listen even more to <u>Jesus</u>! Ask Him to help you to do that.

## Building up
Read about Jesus feeding the 5000 in **John 6v5-13**.

## DAY 7 Mr Cool & Miss Nobody

**KEYPOINT**
The slave girl knew that God could heal Naaman. She told Naaman where to go for help.

Today's passages are:
**Table Talk:** 2 Kings 5v1-8
**XTB:** 2 Kings 5v1-8

**TABLE TALK**

I've called the two main characters in today's story Mr Cool and Miss Nobody. What do you think they're like?

**READ**

*Mr Cool* is called Naaman. As you'll see he's a cool guy. **Read 2 Kings 5v1**

Which of these describes Naaman? **a**—army commander; **b**—highly respected; **c**—brave soldier.

They <u>all</u> describe him! Naaman really is Mr Cool! But what's his problem? (*He has leprosy.*) Leprosy is a nasty disease where your skin goes all lumpy and falls off. Nobody could cure Naaman's leprosy.

*Miss Nobody* was a slave girl. She was an Israelite who'd been captured by Naaman's people, and now worked for Naaman's wife. We don't even know her name—but **she** knew something very important... **Read 2 Kings 5v2-8**

**TALK**

The slave girl knew that God could cure Naaman's leprosy. Who did she tell Naaman to see? (v3) (*The prophet in Samaria.*) Who did she mean? (*Elisha*)

**THINK**

*Mr Cool* couldn't heal himself—he needed help. The ***king of Israel*** didn't help—he panicked! (v7) *Miss Nobody* knew that <u>God</u> could heal Naaman, and she told him where to go to get help.

**PRAY**

Do you ever feel like a 'nobody', like that slave girl? Even so, <u>you</u> can do what she did, and tell people how they can find out more about God. Think of some ways to do this, then ask God to help you.

**Building up**
Check the map on Day 1 to see where **Samaria** was (v3).

---

## DAY 8 Wash in what???

**KEYPOINT**
When Naaman accepted <u>God's</u> way of being cured, he was healed.

Today's passages are:
**Table Talk:** 2 Kings 5v9-14
**XTB:** 2 Kings 5v9-14

**TABLE TALK**

**Recap:** Who was 'Mr Cool' and what was his problem? (*Naaman. He had leprosy.*) Who was 'Miss Nobody' and what did she tell Naaman? (*An Israelite slave girl. She said that Elisha, God's prophet, could cure Naaman.*)

**READ**

Naaman went to Israel to see Elisha. But when he arrived at Elisha's house, Elisha <u>didn't</u> come out to meet him!
**Read 2 Kings 5v9-12**

**TALK**

Elisha sent a servant to Naaman. What was Elisha's message? (v10) (*Go and wash seven times in the Jordan river.*) How did Naaman feel? (v11) (*Angry*)

**READ**

Naaman was furious! Surely God would cure him in a magical, spectacular way—not by dunking in a muddy river! He wasn't going to do what Elisha said. But his servants were much wiser...
**Read 2 Kings 5v13-14**

**TALK**

Naaman's servants persuaded him to wash in the Jordan as he'd been told. What happened? (v14) (*He was healed.*)

This powerful, important ,man had to accept <u>God's</u> way of being cured. When he did, he was healed, just as God's messenger had said.

**PRAY**

Obeying God's words, and living His way, is <u>always</u> the best thing to do—even if His words seem surprising. Ask God to help you to **trust** what He says in the Bible, and **obey** His words, no matter how hard (or odd!) that seems.

**Building up**
Talk about any times when obeying God has been hard, but turned out to be the best.

# DAY 9
# A changed man

**TABLE TALK**

Hide some pieces of paper with these words on: There, is, no, God, in, all, the, world, except, in, Israel. Ask your child to find them and put them in the right order.

Who do you think is speaking? **a**—an Israelite; **b**—Elisha, **c**—an enemy of Israel.

**READ**

These words were spoken by Naaman, the commander of an <u>enemy</u> army! Naaman came from Aram, where they believed in a pretend god called Rimmon. But when Naaman was cured of his leprosy, he realised that **God** is the One True God.
**Read 2 Kings 5v15-19**

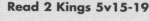

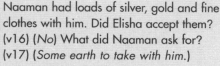
**TALK**

Naaman had loads of silver, gold and fine clothes with him. Did Elisha accept them? (v16) (*No*) What did Naaman ask for? (v17) (*Some earth to take with him.*)

How odd! Maybe Naaman thought he could only pray to <u>Israel's God</u> if he stood on some of <u>Israel's soil</u>! If so, he was wrong. We can pray to God anywhere, anytime.

**THINK**

Think back to the slave girl who told Naaman to go and see Elisha. Her master came home a changed man. Not only was he cured of his leprosy, but he had become a follower of the One True God. How do you think she felt?

**PRAY**

If you tell others about Jesus, they could become Christians too—and you'll have done something everlasting! What a great way to live! Ask God to help you.

## Building up
We can pray to God anywhere, anytime, and about anything! Think of three places you can pray to God, then try and pray in all three today!

# DAY 10
# Gehazi's greed

**TABLE TALK**

**Act out** the next bit of the story:

*As Naaman was leaving in his chariot, Elisha's servant Gehazi chased after him. "Elisha says, 'Two young men have just come to me. Please give them some silver and two sets of clothes.'" Naaman was happy to help, and even gave Gehazi <u>more</u> than he asked for.*

**READ**

Sounds great, doesn't it? Just one small problem. Greedy Gehazi was lying!!!
**Read 2 Kings 5v19-27**

**TALK**

What did Elisha ask Gehazi? (v25) (*"Where have you been?"*) What was Gehazi's answer? (v25) (*He pretended he hadn't been anywhere.*) But Elisha knew the truth! How was Gehazi punished for his greed? (v27) (*He caught Naaman's leprosy.*)

**THINK**

The Bible tells us that **God** gives us everything we have. He gives us <u>good</u> gifts. If we steal, it's like telling God, "You haven't given me enough. I need more!" It shows that we don't <u>trust</u> God to give us everything we need.

Have you ever shoplifted? Or borrowed something and not returned it? Or taken stuff you weren't supposed to? Or dodged a bus fare?

**PRAY**

If you have stolen anything, say **sorry** to God. Ask Him to help you to change. **Thank God** for the good things He has given you. Ask Him to help you to trust Him for everything you need.

## Building up
Read **Psalm 23** together. Thank God for all the good gifts listed in this psalm.

# DAY 11
## Why did God...?

**TABLE TALK**

Put some objects on the table (eg: apple, key, coin, rubber duck...) Ask your child if they will float or sink. (If you can, try this out with a bowl of water.) In today's story, something floats that shouldn't!

**READ**

Elisha was the leader of a group of prophets (God's messengers). But their meeting hall was starting to get overcrowded... **Read 2 Kings 6v1-7**

What happened to the axe-head? (v5) (*It fell into the water.*) Why was the man so upset? (v5) (*He'd borrowed it.*) In those days an iron axe-head was expensive. What did Elisha do? (v6) (*Made the axe-head float.*)

**THINK**

Sometimes, Bible stories can be hard to understand. An older Christian may be able to explain it, or another part of the Bible may tell you about it. But sometimes we <u>don't know</u> why something happened! In that case, the best thing to do is think carefully about what we <u>do know</u>:

**1.** Who were the people in the story?
  **a)** God's enemies
  **b)** God's followers

**2.** What is God like?
  **a)** He is kind and loving
  **b)** He is cruel and mean

**3.** What can God do?
  **a)** He can do anything
  **b)** He can only do some things

The answers are **b,a,a**. God can do **anything**, so making iron float is easy for Him. And God loves to be **kind** to His followers. Maybe that's why He made the axe-head float, because He cared about the man's sadness.

**PRAY**

God loves to be kind to **you** too. Thank Him for His HUGE kindness to you.

---

# DAY 12
## Who's the King?

**TABLE TALK**

**Draw** a large crown. What would you like best and least about being a king or queen?

Being king probably feels pretty powerful. But the king of Aram (Syria) was about to find out that he didn't have much power at all... Read the cartoon story in **Notes for Parents** opposite.

**READ**

Read the verses to see what happened next. **Read 2 Kings 6v18-23**

**TALK**

What did Elisha pray would happen to the enemy soldiers? (v18) (*They would become blind.*) What city did he lead them to? (v19) (*Samaria*) God opened their eyes again so that they could see. The king of Israel wanted to kill the soldiers, but what did Elisha tell him to do instead? (v22) (*Give them a feast, then send them back to their master, the king of Aram.*)

The king of Aram <u>thought</u> he was in control, but he wasn't! Copy the letters hidden in the cartoon story to see why.

**God is the** _ _ _ _ _ _ _ _

**DO**

Write 'God is the Real King' on your picture of a crown. Display it where you will all see it this week.

**PRAY**

God is the King of everything. He is always in control. Thank Him for this.

### Building up
**Psalm 2** shows how foolish it is for human kings to try to beat God! Read it together.

# DAY 12
## Notes for Parents

he king of Aram
went to war
gainst Israel.

But his plans didn't work out...

...because Elisha kept warning
the king of Israel!

le made plans to attack God's
eople, the Israelites.

The king of Aram was furious!

Find out where
Elisha is, so that I
can capture him.

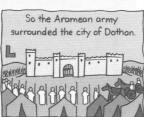

So the Aramean army
surrounded the city of Dothan.

Elisha's servant was scared
when he saw the army.

What shall
we do?

But Elisha told him not to be
afraid.

Those who are
with us are more
than those who
are with them.

hen Elisha asked God to show
s servant the truth.

O Lord, open
his eyes so that
he may see.

And the servant saw the hills full
of horses and chariots of fire!

Taken from 2 Kings 6v8-17.

### Building up (Day 13)

(Note for parents: This part of the story may be too distressing for your child.) The people in Samaria were desperate—read **2 Kings 6v26-33**. The king of Israel was in despair. Even so, what he says in v27 is right. Who is the <u>only</u> One who can help us in hopeless situations? (The LORD.) Are you despairing or in trouble right now? Turn to God for help. He is always able to help, and will do what is good and right.

# DAY 13
## The siege of Samaria

**KEYPOINT**
God is the Real King. That means God is in control and His words always come true.

Today's passages are:
**Table Talk:** 2 Kings 6v24-25; 7v1-2
**XTB:** 2 Kings 6v24-7v2

**TABLE TALK**

What did you put on yesterday's crown? (*God is the Real King*) What does that mean? (*God is in control.*) Today we'll meet three people who need to learn that:

**1** <u>The King of Aram</u>. Ben-Hadad, king of Aram, attacked Israel and its capital city Samaria... **Read 2 Kings 6v24-25**

**TALK**

What is a siege? (*When an army circles a walled city to trap the people inside.*) Because of the siege, the food was running out in Samaria and the people were starving. Food had become terribly expensive. How much did a donkey's head cost? (v25) (*80 pieces of silver.*)

**2** <u>The king of Israel</u>. The king was trapped inside Samaria too. When he saw how the people were suffering, he blamed Elisha, and even planned to kill him! (v26-33) But Elisha had a message for the king. **Read 2 Kings 7v1-2**

**TALK**

Elisha said there'd be plenty of cheap food in Samaria again. When would that happen? (v1) (*Tomorrow*)

**3** <u>The Israelite officer</u>. This officer was the messenger for the king of Israel. But he <u>didn't believe</u> Elisha! So what did Elisha tell him about the promised food? (v2) (*He'd see it but not eat any of it.*)

Elisha wasn't speaking his <u>own</u> words. Whose words were they? (v1) (*God's*)

**PRAY**

The king's messenger didn't believe God's words. Do <u>you</u> sometimes find it hard to believe God's words in the Bible? Talk about this, and ask God to help you.

**Building up** See Notes for Parents opposite.

# DAY 14
## Good news!

**KEYPOINT**
The four men knew they mustn't keep the good news to themselves. We mustn't either!

Today's passages are:
**Table Talk**: 2 Kings 7v3-11
**XTB**: 2 Kings 7v3-11

**TABLE TALK**

**Recap:** Who had attacked Israel?—the Americans or the Arameans? Was the city of Samaria under siege or under water? When did Elisha say there'd be plenty of cheap food?—tomorrow or next week? Whose words was Elisha speaking?—his own or God's?

**READ**

That evening, four men with leprosy decided to leave the city and go to the enemy camp... **Read 2 Kings 7v3-11**

**TALK**

What did the men find when they reached the enemy camp? (v5) (*No one*) Why had the Arameans left? (v6) (*God made them hear the sound of a large army.*) For a while, the men grabbed everything they could. But then they decided to go back to the city. Why? (v9) (*They had good news and knew they shouldn't keep it to themselves.*)

**THINK**

These four men had **good news** to share. They knew it would be wrong to keep it to themselves. If you're a Christian (a follower of Jesus) then you have good news to share too! What is it? (*The good news that Jesus came as our Rescuer, so that we can be friends with God.*)

**PRAY**

Think of some ways that you can share the good news about Jesus with your friends. Ask God to help you to do that this week.

### Building up
'Gospel' is a Greek word that means 'Good News'. **Read Mark 1v1**. Why do you think the first four books in the Bible (Matthew, Mark, Luke and John) are called Gospels?

# DAY 15
## The promise keeper

**KEYPOINT**
God's words always come true —His promises and His warnings.

Today's passages are:
**Table Talk**: 2 Kings 7v12-20
**XTB**: 2 Kings 7v12-20

**TABLE TALK**

God had given a **promise**: that there would be plenty of cheap food tomorrow. And a **warning**: that the king's messenger (who didn't believe the promise) would see the food but not eat any of it. Do you think God's words would come true? Why/why not?

**READ**

The four men with leprosy came back to the town and told their good news that the enemy army had gone. But the king of Israel didn't believe it! He thought the Arameans were trying to trick him...
**Read 2 Kings 7v12-16**

**TALK**

Had the Arameans gone away? (v15) (*Yes*) Was there plenty of cheap food? (v16) (*Yes*)

God **promised** that there'd be plenty of cheap food for His people to eat—and there was. *Just as God said!*

But God had given a **warning** too—to the king's messenger who didn't believe God's promise.
**Read 2 Kings 7v17-20**

Did God's warning come true? (v17) (*Yes*)

**THINK**

God's words **always** come true—His promises and His warnings. How does that make you feel?

**PRAY**

Talk to God about this—and remember that you can always trust God to do what's right and good.

### Building up
Check out some of God's other promises and warnings: read Romans 10v13, Hebrews 13v5, 1 Corinthians 10v13 and Isaiah 13v11.

# DAYS 16 – 35
## Notes for Parents

### MEET JOHN

**John** was one of Jesus' closest friends (called **disciples**). His brother James was also a disciple.

John wrote a book all about Jesus. It's called **John's Gospel**. The word 'gospel' means 'good news'. John wrote his book to tell us the good news about *Jesus*.

John also wrote four other Bible books. They are *Revelation*, *1 John*, *2 John* and *3 John*.

### WHY DID JOHN WRITE A BOOK?

At the end of his book, John tells us why he wrote it. (It's in John 20v31).

> So that you may believe that Jesus is the Christ, the Son of God, and that by believing you may have life in His name.

John wants us to believe that Jesus is the Christ (Messiah). That means God's chosen King.

In his book, John tells us loads of amazing things that Jesus did and said.

They are all *signposts* pointing to who Jesus is. They help us understand more about Jesus.

# DAY 16
## Light and wrong

**KEYPOINT**
Jesus is the Christ (God's chosen King). He can cure illness and forgive our horrible sin.

Today's passages are:
**Table Talk:** John 9v1-7
**XTB:** John 9v1-7

**TABLE TALK**

Welcome to John's book about Jesus. In it we'll see Jesus ride a donkey, make a blind man see and raise a friend back to life! And we'll also read some of the amazing things Jesus said.

Find out more about John in **Notes for Parents**.

**READ**

In today's story, Jesus and His disciples meet a blind man. **Read John 9v1-5**

**TALK**

The disciples thought blindness was a punishment from God. What did they ask Jesus? (v2) (*Was it his sin or his parents' sin that made him blind.*) But what reason did <u>Jesus</u> give? (v3) (*So that God's work could be seen in his life.*) Jesus was going to do something amazing for this man so that people could see **God** at work!

**THINK**

What did Jesus call Himself? (v5) (*The light of the world.*) If we don't know and love Jesus it's as if we are **blind**. We <u>can't see</u> that we've sinned and need Jesus to forgive us. Jesus is the **light** who shows us the way to be forgiven.

**DO**

Read what happened next in **John 9v6-7** and act it out.

Wow! The man obeyed what Jesus told him to do, and he was able to see!

**PRAY**

If people trust Jesus and do what He says, they can have their sins forgiven. Thank Jesus that He can cure illness and forgive our horrible sin.

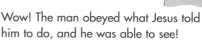

### Building up
There are seven 'I AM' sayings in John's Gospel. Check them all out in Notes for Parents on Day 20.

## DAY 17
# Who is Jesus?

**KEYPOINT**
The healed man and the Pharisees disagreed about who Jesus was. What do <u>you</u> say?

Today's passages are:
**Table Talk:** John 9v13-17
**XTB:** John 9v8-23

**TABLE TALK**

<u>Note:</u> Please read the whole of chapter 9 beforehand, so that you can sum up the story for your child.

<u>Recap:</u> In yesterday's story, Jesus healed a blind man with the world's first mud pack! Ask your child to tell you the story.

**READ**

Everyone who knew the man wanted to know <u>who</u> had healed him (v8-12). But the Pharisees (Jewish leaders) were not so excited about Jesus...
**Read John 9v13-17**

**TALK**

What day was it? (v14) (*The Sabbath, the Jewish day of rest.*) Some of the Pharisees said Jesus <u>couldn't</u> have come from God. Why not? (v16) (*Because He worked on God's rest day.*) But doing good and healing someone on the Sabbath wasn't wrong! So some Pharisees thought Jesus was a <u>good man</u> (v16).

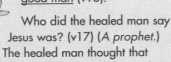

Who did the healed man say Jesus was? (v17) (*A prophet.*) The healed man thought that Jesus was a messenger sent by God. He was half right! But he didn't yet realise that Jesus was the special King sent by God to rescue His people.

**PRAY**

Who do <u>you</u> think Jesus is? If you believe God sent Jesus to rescue you, thank God for sending Jesus.

### Building up
**Read John 9v18-23.** Most of the Pharisees refused to believe that Jesus was sent by God, even after they had spoken to the healed man's parents! Pray for anyone you know who doesn't believe what the Bible says about Jesus.

---

## DAY 18
# Blinding truth

**KEYPOINT**
The healed man spoke up about the things he knew about Jesus. So should we.

Today's passages are:
**Table Talk:** John 9v24-34
**XTB:** John 9v24-34

**TABLE TALK**

(*You need pencil and paper.*) Copy these sentences from the story onto six strips of paper. As you read today's verses, divide the sentences into two sets—words spoken by the **Pharisees** (Jewish leaders) and words spoken by the **healed man**.

- 'We know this man is a sinner.'
- 'I was blind, but now I see.'
- 'Do you want to become his disciples?'
- 'We are disciples of Moses.'
- 'We don't even know where he comes from.'
- 'If this man were not from God, he could do nothing.'

**READ**

**Read John 9v24-34**

**TALK**

The Pharisees were important, powerful men. They wanted the healed man to agree that Jesus was a sinner (v24) and couldn't have been sent by God (v29). Why do you think the healed man refused to agree with them?

The healed man didn't know much about Jesus yet. But he worked out that Jesus must be from God, because He could do things that only **God** could do. Sadly, the Pharisees refused to believe the evidence.

**THINK**

The healed man didn't know everything about Jesus. But he spoke up about the things he DID know. How about <u>you</u>? What could you tell somebody else about Jesus?

**PRAY**

Ask God to help you to be ready to speak up for Jesus whenever you can.

### Building up
What are Jesus' miracles like? (*Signposts*) **Read John 20v30-31** again. This miracle was a signpost too—but the Pharisees still refused to believe.

# DAY 19
# The big choice

**KEYPOINT**
The man's spiritual eyes have been opened—he now sees <u>who</u> Jesus is and believes in Him.

Today's passages are:
**Table Talk:** John 9v35-38
**XTB:** John 9v35-41

**TABLE TALK**

**Recap:** What did the healed man believe about Jesus? (*He came from God.*) What did the Pharisees say about Jesus? (*He was a sinner who couldn't be from God.*)

**READ**

Jesus found the healed man and talked to him. As you read today's verses, listen for two names for Jesus.
**Read John 9v35-38**

**TALK**

What was the <u>first</u> name given to Jesus? (v35) (*'The Son of Man'. This title is used in Daniel 7v13-14 to refer to the Messiah [Christ]—Jesus often used it to refer to Himself.*) What was the <u>second</u> name for Jesus? (v38) (*'Lord'*)

**THINK**

Look back to v11 to see what the healed man first called Jesus. (*'The man called Jesus.'*) Now, this man is calling Jesus 'Lord'. His <u>physical eyes</u> have been opened—he can see. And his <u>spiritual eyes</u> have been opened too—he now sees **who** Jesus is and believes in Him.

Talk about ways each of you has come to see Jesus more clearly. (*This may be a good time for an adult to explain how they became a Christian, and why.*)

**PRAY**

Thank God for opening your eyes so that you can see who Jesus is.

### Building up
**Read John 9v39-41**. The Pharisees thought they could **see**. They thought they knew the truth about God. But they didn't because they refused to **see** that **Jesus is God**. But some people realise they are blind and need Jesus to rescue them from their blind sinful ways. There are only two choices. Believe in Jesus, and live His way. Or have nothing to do with Jesus. Ask God to help you make the right choice.

# DAY 20
# Great gate

**KEYPOINT**
Jesus is the gate—the <u>only way</u> to be saved and to have eternal life in heaven.

Today's passages are:
**Table Talk:** John 10v1-10
**XTB:** John 10v1-10

**DO**

(*You need pencil and paper.*) Each draw a sheep. As you draw, talk about how a shepherd looks after his sheep.

**READ**

Today, Jesus says He is both a shepherd and a gate! **Read John 10v1-6**

Who will the sheep listen to?—the shepherd or the thief? (v3) Will they ever follow a stranger? (v5) (*No!*)

**THINK**

Some religious leaders (like the Pharisees) tried to lead people away from God. Like a thief trying to take sheep the wrong way. But true followers of Jesus will only follow Him. He shows them the right way to live. They won't follow anyone else.

**READ**

### Read John 10v7-10

What will happen for those who 'come in through Jesus'? (v9) (*They will be saved.*)
Look at the sheep pen picture. How many ways into the sheep pen are there?

You can only get in through the **gate**. It is the **only way**.

**THINK**

Jesus, the gate, is the **only way** to become friends with God. The **only way** to be saved (have your sins forgiven—v9). The **only way** to eternal life in heaven (v10).

**PRAY**

Thank Jesus for each of these things.

### Building up
In Bible times, some sheep pens didn't have a wooden gate at all. They just had a gap. When the shepherd brought his sheep into the pen for the night, he then lay down and slept in the gap. He <u>was</u> the gate!

# DAY 20
## Notes for Parents

### THE 'I AM' SAYINGS

There are seven 'I am' sayings in John's Gospel, where Jesus uses picture language to help us understand more about who He is and why He came.

'I am the bread of life.' John 6v35

'I am the light of the world.'
John 8v12

'I am the gate.'　　　John 10v7

'I am the good shepherd.'
John 10v11

'I am the resurrection and the life.'
John 11v25

'I am the way, the truth and the life.'　　　John 14v6

'I am the vine.'　　John 15v5

# DAY 21
## The good shepherd

Today's passages are:
**Table Talk:** John 10v11-15
**XTB:** John 10v11-15

 **DO**
Play **hangman** to guess the phrase 'Good Shepherd.'

 **READ**
In today's verses Jesus tells us that He is our Good Shepherd. Read the verses to find out why. **Read John 10v11-15**

 **TALK**
What does the hired man do when a wolf attacks the sheep? (v12) (*He runs away!*) Why? (v13) (*He doesn't care about the sheep.*) But the good shepherd knows and loves his sheep! What is he ready to do for them? (v11&15) (*Die for them.*)

**THINK**
Jesus' followers (Christians) are like sheep. And Jesus is the good Shepherd who cares for them. He loves His sheep so much He was even ready to die for them! Read 'The Lost Sheep' in **Notes for Parents** opposite to find out why.

Jesus died to rescue anyone who trusts in Him. And we can get to know Jesus really really well. We can be close to Jesus, just as He is close to His Father, God. (That's what v14-15 mean.)

 **PRAY**
If you want to be Jesus' friend, tell Him right now.

### Building up
Jesus our Shepherd is thrilled when someone who is lost comes to Him to be saved. In fact, there's a party in heaven to celebrate! Read Jesus' story about this in **Luke 15v1-7.**

### THE LOST SHEEP

Imagine a sheep that has wandered away from the rest of the flock, and got itself stuck on a mountain ledge. What will happen if it isn't rescued? (*It will become weak and eventually die.*)

The Bible says that all of us are like sheep, going our own way, instead of following Jesus, the Good Shepherd. That's called **sin**. A lost sheep will die because it has left the shepherd's care. We too will die, far away from God's love forever.

A sheep can't find its shepherd. It needs to be rescued. So do we!

### JESUS IS OUR RESCUER

The great news is that Jesus came to **rescue** us from our sins. At the first Easter, Jesus was nailed to a cross and left to die. As He died, Jesus rescued us from sin by taking all the punishment we deserve.

Did you know that God must punish the way we live? That's because we make His world bad and sad. But when He died, Jesus was punished **instead of us**, so we can be forgiven.

That's why Jesus said, *"I am the good shepherd. The good shepherd lays down his life for the sheep."* (John 10v11)

**KEYPOINT**
All Christians are in one big family, because they've all been rescued by Jesus.

Today's passages are:
**Table Talk:** John 10v16
**XTB:** John 10v16-18

 **DO** (*You need pencil and paper.*) Each draw a picture of someone in your family. Can the others guess who it is?

 **READ** Jesus, the Good Shepherd, is still talking about '<u>sheep</u>'. But He's really talking about <u>people</u>... **Read John 10v16**

 **TALK** The people listening to Jesus were Jewish. They were God's special people and thought they would be the <u>only ones</u> who would be with God in heaven. In other words, they thought they were the only 'sheep' following the Good Shepherd. But what did Jesus say? (v16) (*He had other sheep as well.*)

Jesus didn't come to rescue only Jewish people, but people from all backgrounds and parts of the world.

How many flocks will Jesus have? (v16) (*Just one, with one shepherd.*) Jesus is the Good Shepherd, who looks after His sheep, Christians. All Christians are in **one big family**, because they've all been **rescued by Jesus!**

**PRAY** Think of some Christians you know about in other countries. They're all part of God's big family! Pray for them, asking God to look after them and help them to serve Him.

 **PRAY**

 **DO** Why not write to some of them to tell them you are praying for them?

### Building up
**Read John 10v17-18**. Why does God love Jesus? (v17) (*Because He chose to die for sinners like us.*) So God gave Jesus power, not only to give up His life to rescue us, but to come alive again and beat sin, death and the devil.

# DAY 23
## Flock tactics

Today's passages are:
**Table Talk:** John 10v27-30
**XTB:** John 10v19-30

**TABLE TALK**

**DO**

Put a bunch of keys on the table (the noisier the better!) and close your eyes. Challenge your child to pick up the keys and hide them without you hearing.

**READ**

If you are quiet and careful you can snatch the keys away. But Jesus our Shepherd promises that **no one** can snatch His sheep away from Him!
**Read John 10v27-30**

**TALK**

Jesus promises three fantastic things for everyone who follows Him. Can you spot them?

(*1—v27, Jesus knows us. We are His friends. 2—v28, He gives us eternal life. We will live with Jesus forever in heaven. 3—v27, No one can snatch us away from Jesus.*)

**THINK**

*Wow!* Talk about those three promises. How does each one make you feel? What do you want to say to Jesus?

Now pray together about your answers.

**PRAY**

### Building up
**Read John 10v30 again**. Compare this verse with **John 14v8-11**. Do you want to know what God is like? You can find out by looking at Jesus!

# DAY 24
## Jesus is God

Today's passages are:
**Table Talk:** John 10v31-33&37-38
**XTB:** John 10v31-42

**TABLE TALK**

Yesterday's verses ended with Jesus saying, "I and the Father are one." (v30) Who is 'the Father'? (*God*) So Jesus is saying that He is God!

**DO**

(*You need paper and scissors.*)
Write **'Is Jesus God?'** on the paper. Today's verses will help us to answer that question. **Read John 10v31-33**

**TALK**

What did the Jewish people want to do to Jesus? (v31) (*Stone Him to death.*) Why? (v33) (*For saying He is God.*) These Jews thought that Jesus was only a <u>man</u> who was trying to make Himself <u>God</u>. This was a very bad sin called blasphemy.

**READ**

Let's see how Jesus answers the question. **Read John 10v37-38**

Jesus said they mustn't believe Him unless He did what? (v37) (*Unless He did what His Father [God] did.*) Did Jesus do things that only God can do? (*Yes!*) So, should the people believe that Jesus was God? (*Yes*)

**DO**

So what is the answer to the question 'Is Jesus God?'. Cut up the paper and rearrange the words to show the answer: **'Jesus is God!'**

**PRAY**

Do **you** believe that Jesus is God? Think about what He has done and said. God won't wait for your decision forever, so ask Him to help you believe now.

### Building up
**Read John 10v39-42**. Despite everything these people had seen and heard, they still wouldn't believe that Jesus was God! So Jesus went where people **would** believe Him.

## THE DEATH OF LAZARUS

We're going to spend the next five days looking at this story. You will find it helpful to read the whole of chapter 11 first so that you're familiar with it.

**Talking about death with children**
Children may have loads of questions about death and heaven: 'Where is heaven?', 'How old will I be in heaven?', 'Will I be an angel?', 'Will there be animals in heaven?'.

The Bible tells us that Jesus has prepared a special place for us in heaven:

*'In my Father's house are many rooms; if it were not so I would have told you. I am going there to prepare a place for you.' John 14v2*

We can assure children that heaven will be the best it can possibly be. But the Bible doesn't really tell us much about it—we will have to wait and see. So it's OK not to know the answers to all their questions!

Talking to children about death can be tricky. It so depends on what kind of question they ask, and why they are asking. Your local Christian bookshop will stock a range of booklets designed to help children think about death. You may find some of these helpful. Or ask other Christian parents how they have answered similar questions.

As we look at the death and resurrection of Lazarus, there will be opportunities to explain the Christian view of death, and the certainty we can have if we are followers of Jesus. Be sure that your children understand that being with Jesus in heaven will be wonderful, and is a sure promise for all those who have put their trust in Him.

 **KEYPOINT**
Jesus waited before going to Lazarus because He had something better planned.

Today's passages are:
**Table Talk:** John 11v3-6
**XTB:** John 11v1-16

**TABLE TALK**

Read the cartoon above. How do you think Joe felt at first? How did he feel when he found his friends had something better planned?

**READ**

Lazarus, and his sisters Mary and Martha, were Jesus' friends. When Lazarus became very ill, his sisters sent Jesus a message. **Read John 11v3-6**

**TALK**

Did Jesus go to see Lazarus straight away? (*No!*) How long did He wait? (v6) (*2 days*) Jesus said this had happened so that someone would be glorified. Who? (v4) (*God and God's Son, Jesus.*) We'll find out what happened tomorrow...

**THINK**

**Could** Jesus have healed Lazarus? (*Yes!*) But He didn't—because He had something better planned.
**Could** God answer all our prayers? (*Yes!*) But sometimes He says No, or asks us to wait, because He has something better planned.

**PRAY**

It can be hard to trust that God always does what's best. Ask Him to help you.

### Building Up
After waiting two days, Jesus said it was time to go to Lazarus. **Read John 11v14-15**. Lazarus had died, but Jesus said He was glad that He hadn't been there! Why? (v15) (*So that His disciples would believe.*)

# DAY 26
## Dead serious

Today's passages are:
**Table Talk:** John 11v17-27
**XTB:** John 11v17-27

**Recap yesterday's story:** Who was dying? (*Lazarus*) Who sent the message to Jesus? (*Mary and Martha*) How long did Jesus wait? (*Two days*)

By the time Jesus arrived, Lazarus had been dead for **four days**. Jesus was about to do an amazing miracle. But first He had something very important to say to Martha (and to us!). **Read John 11v17-27**

Verse 25 is another of Jesus' 'I am' sayings. (The full list is in Notes for Parents on Day 20.) What does Jesus say He is? (*The resurrection and the life.*) 'Resurrection' means a dead person coming back to life.

Jesus said that anyone 'who believes in Him will live, even though he dies' (v25). What do you think He meant? (*Life here on earth **ends**. Our body dies—we don't need it any more. But life in heaven with Jesus **never ends!** We will have new bodies—and never be ill or in pain. This is a promise for everyone who believes in Jesus—and Jesus always keeps His promises!*)

If you are followers of Jesus, then you can look forward to a wonderful home in heaven with Him. Thank Him for this.

### Building up
Sometimes people worry about death. Why do Jesus' words help us not to be scared of dying? (*See **Notes for Parents** yesterday for help on talking with children about death.*)

# DAY 27
## Sad sister

Today's passages are:
**Table Talk:** John 11v28-37
**XTB:** John 11v28-37

Mary and Martha are Lazarus' sisters. Martha has already gone to meet Jesus. Now it's Mary's turn.
**Read John 11v28-31**

Did Mary go to see Jesus straight away, or did she wait? (v29&31) (*She went quickly.*)

When Mary heard that Jesus was there she rushed to meet Him. Are **you** like that? Do you love to spend time talking to Jesus? Do you do it every day?

**Read John 11v32-37**

Verse 35 is the shortest verse in the Bible. What does it say? (*Jesus wept.*) Wow! Jesus is the Life. He <u>knew</u> Lazarus would be O.K. But He still wept! Death is our great enemy and Jesus knows and cares for how we feel—even though He's beaten death!

Jesus is a great example to us. He showed sympathy to Mary, and we should show sympathy to people who are sad. Think of some people you know who are sad. How can you show sympathy and friendship to them?

Ask God to comfort the people you've thought of. And ask Him to help you to show them sympathy and friendship.

### Building up
What question did people ask in v37? (*'He opened the eyes of the blind man. Couldn't He have kept Lazarus from dying?'*) The answer is Yes! So why didn't Jesus do that? (Check your answer in **John 11v4&15**.)

# DAY 28
## Life saver

**KEYPOINT**
Jesus brought Lazarus back to life to bring glory to God and so that people would believe in Him.

Today's passages are:
**Table Talk:** John 11v38-44
**XTB:** John 11v38-44

**TABLE TALK**

Think back to the beginning of the story. How long did Jesus wait? (*Two days*) Jesus didn't rush to cure Lazarus because He had something <u>better</u> planned. Do you know (or can you guess!) what it was?

**READ**

Lazarus was buried in a cave—sealed with a huge stone. He had been dead for four days, and his body was starting to smell! Yuck! But Jesus was about to do something incredible...
**Read John 11v38-44**

**TALK**

What was the first thing Jesus did after the stone was taken away? (v41) (*He prayed.*) After speaking to God, Jesus spoke to Lazarus! What happened when Jesus told Lazarus to come out of the tomb? (v44) (*He did!*) Dead bodies were

usually wrapped in strips of cloth before burial, so what did Jesus tell the people to do? (v44) (*Unwrap him.*)

Verse 40 tells us why Jesus did this amazing miracle. (*So that they would see God's glory.*) Verse 42 tells us the other reason. (*So that they would believe that God sent Jesus.*)

**PRAY**

Thank God that **all** Jesus' followers will come alive again in heaven—with better bodies than Lazarus and forever!

### Building up
Food for thought: Why did Jesus call Lazarus by name? (v43) The Bible doesn't tell us, but perhaps it's because Jesus is so powerful that if He hadn't given a name, every dead body in the area would have come back to life!

# DAY 29
## Perfect plan

**KEYPOINT**
Caiaphas prophesied that one man (Jesus) would die for the people. He was right!

Today's passages are:
**Table Talk:** John 11v45-50
**XTB:** John 11v45-57

**TABLE TALK**

Think again about yesterday's story. How would you have felt if you had seen Lazarus come out of the tomb? What would you have thought of Jesus?

**READ**

Many of the people who saw Jesus bring Lazarus back to life put their faith in Jesus. But the Jewish leaders were worried that Jesus would become hugely popular and that the Romans might even destroy the Jewish nation!
**Read John 11v45-50**

**TALK**

The high priest was called Caiaphas. What did he say? (v50) (*It is better for one man to die than the whole nation be destroyed.*) What Caiaphas said had **two** very different meanings:

**1**—What did Caiaphas mean that the Jewish leaders should do? (*Kill Jesus to <u>save</u> the Jews from being destroyed by the Romans—see v53.*)

**2**—But what else does 'one man dying for the people' mean? (*Jesus' death would <u>save</u> people, but not from the Romans. It would save people from being punished for their sins.*)

**THINK**

From that day the Jewish leaders plotted to kill Jesus (v53). But God used their **wicked plot** to carry out His **wonderful plan** to rescue people!

**PRAY**

Thank God for His wonderful rescue plan.

### Building up
When people acted on their <u>wicked plot</u> to kill Jesus, they were actually carrying out God's <u>wonderful plan</u>. Read how Peter explains this in **Acts 2v22-24** and **Acts 4v27-28**.

# DAY 30
# Mary's hairy story

 **KEYPOINT**
Mary showed her love by washing Jesus' feet with perfume and drying them with her hair.

Today's passages are:
**Table Talk:** John 12v1-8
**XTB:** John 12v1-11

 **DO** Try some different perfumes or aftershave, and decide which you like best.

 **READ** Jesus went back to visit Lazarus and his sisters, Mary and Martha. While he was there Mary did something surprising with some very expensive perfume. **Read John 12v1-8**

 **TALK** What did Mary do with the perfume? (v3) (*Poured it on Jesus' feet.*) Look at the picture to see how she was able to reach His feet.

What did she wipe His feet with? (*Her hair.*) Who complained about her using such expensive perfume this way? (v4) (*Judas*) But Jesus knew that He would soon die and that Mary had done a lovely thing for Him before He died.

 **THINK** Only slaves would usually wash dusty, stinky feet. And not with their hair! But Mary loved Jesus so much that she washed His dusty feet using very expensive perfume! Think of some things that **you** can do to show how much you love Jesus. (*Eg: talking to Him more, telling people about Him, showing love to people in need...*)

 **PRAY** Ask God to help you to do the things you have thought about.

## Building up
The Jewish leaders were already plotting to kill Jesus. But their plot became even worse: **read John 12v9-11**.

# DAY 31
# Return of the King!

 **KEYPOINT**
King Jesus rode into Jerusalem on a donkey, just as Zechariah had prophesied.

Today's passages are:
**Table Talk:** John 12v12-16
**XTB:** John 12v12-19

 **TABLE TALK** How many ways could you travel into the middle of town? (*Eg: bus, walk, pogo-stick...*)

 **READ** When Jesus arrived in Jerusalem, He rode in on a young donkey. **Read John 12v12-16**

 **TALK** The people of Jerusalem all shouted and cheered for Jesus. What did they call Him? (v13) (*King of Israel.*) They were **right** that Jesus was their King. But they thought He should be a mighty warrior who would bash the Romans. They were **wrong** about that!

 **THINK** What kind of King had Jesus come to be? (*Jesus was the promised Christ, which means 'God's chosen King'. But He was a Servant King, who came to die for His people. He would save them from <u>sin</u>—not the <u>Romans</u>!*)

 **PRAY** Spend time praising Jesus the King and thanking Him for coming to rescue us.

## Building up
Instead of a warhorse, King Jesus rode on a young donkey—just as the prophet Zechariah had said 500 years earlier. Zechariah said the promised king would *bring peace*, *rule the earth* and *free prisoners*. Look out for these things as you read **Zechariah 9v9-11**. Jesus died on the cross to *bring peace* to the world and to free people who are *prisoners to sin*. One day He will *rule* everyone everywhere.

## DAY 32
# Seeds of truth

**KEYPOINT**
Jesus teaches four top truths, two about Himself, and two about how we should live.

Today's passages are:
**Table Talk:** John 12v20-26
**XTB:** John 12v20-26

**DO**

Write out these four **top truths**:

**A**—Jesus came for the whole world.
**B**—We must serve Jesus.
**C**—Jesus' death gives life.
**D**—We must love God, not life.

As you read today's verses, match them to each top truth:

**ONE**

**Read John 12v20-22**
Where did these men come from? (*Greece*) These Greeks show us that Jesus didn't just come for Jewish people, but Gentiles (non-Jews) too. Which truth is that? (*Truth A*)

**TWO**

**Read John 12v23-24**
A seed must fall from a plant and **die** before a new plant can grow from it. Jesus knew that He would soon **die**. But His death will bring everlasting **life** to anyone who turns to Him for forgiveness. Which truth is that? (*Truth C*)

**THREE**

**Read John 12v25**
People who live to please themselves, instead of God, will be punished. But people who put God first will live with Him for ever! Which truth? (*Truth D*)

**FOUR**

**Read John 12v26**
If you're serious about following Jesus, then you've got to show it in the way you live your life. It pleases God when we do. Which truth is that? (*Truth B*)

**PRAY**

Thank God for truths A and C. Ask Him to help you do B and D.

### Building up
We are to serve Jesus. He was a servant too!
**Read Mark 10v42-45.**

## DAY 33
# Why did Jesus die?

**KEYPOINT**
Jesus came to earth to die. His death brought glory to God—and also to Jesus Himself.

Today's passages are:
**Table Talk:** John 12v27-33
**XTB:** John 12v27-36

**TABLE TALK**

What do we call the day Jesus died? (*Good Friday*) What an odd name! Jesus died a horrible, painful death. So why do we call it 'good'? (*Because Jesus did such a good thing in dying for us so that we can have our sins forgiven.*)

**READ**

In today's verses, Jesus hasn't died yet. But He knows He will die soon, and is talking about His death.
**Read John 12v27-33**

**TALK**

In v27 Jesus says that His reason for coming to earth was to **die**! What three things would His death do? (v31-32)

**1**—Judge the world (v31). People who turn to Jesus for forgiveness will be rescued from sin. Those who don't will be punished by God.

**2**—Beat the devil (v31). When Jesus died and was raised back to life, the devil was defeated!

**3**—Draw all people to Jesus (v32). Jesus' death made it possible for anyone to be forgiven and become Jesus' friend.

**PRAY**

Jesus' death brought glory to God (v28)—and also to Jesus Himself. He deserves all of our praise too. What do you want to thank and praise Him for?

### Building up
To find out more, send for the free booklet **Why did Jesus die?**. Write to *Table Talk, The Good Book Company, 37 Elm Road, New Malden, Surrey, KT3 3HB* or email me: *alison@thegoodbook.co.uk*

**'Children, obey your parents...'**
(Ephesians 6v1) What a popular verse for mums and dads everywhere! Good for meal times, great for bed times, and a wonderful one-liner for when granny and grandpa come to stay.

But Ephesians 6v1 goes with 6v4. Paul goes on to say: **'Fathers, do not exasperate your children; instead bring them up in the training and instruction of the Lord'**. (Eph 6v4) Ah! That puts a slightly different complexion on things.

It's just like that section only a few verses earlier: 'wives, submit to your husbands'. It seems a bit one-sided, until we go on to read 'husbands, love your wives, just as Christ loved the church'. Seeing how Christ loved the church enough to die a humiliating death on her behalf, maybe husbands don't have it so easy after all...

Anyway, back to children and parents. Or, more specifically (and intriguingly), children and <u>fathers</u>. In v4, Paul addresses fathers. Perhaps Paul suspected that fathers are more inclined to be exasperating. Perhaps he knew that fathers are often too happy or too busy to leave the training and instructing of the Lord to mothers. Well, if so, things haven't changed much.

Now this isn't to get mothers off the hook. This isn't an excuse for mothers to ignore their instructing duties. Many mothers simply do not have the choice, because Dad is absent, or else not interested in spiritual things. And it certainly isn't a licence for maternal exasperation at their thoroughly annoying offspring! Mums have a God-given responsibility to help and support their children's fathers in the bringing up of the children. So if you are a mother reading this, perhaps you'd like to push this article

(gently!) under the nose of the nearest father—as well as taking note of it for yourself.

But why does Paul write specifically to fathers? I think there are at least three reasons.

## 1. RESPONSIBILITY

The Scriptures are clear that fathers are to have the ultimate responsibility in the home. This does not mean that they should do everything like a power-crazed control-freak. Nor does it means that they should sit back, delegate everything, and enjoy The Simpsons. But it does mean that fathers will be answerable before God for the state of their family. If a father sets a tone of exasperation and frustration in the family—through his own inconsistency or unrealistic expectations—then that will appear in the rest of the family's lives. If a father doesn't take seriously the responsibility of encouraging spiritual growth in his children, then they will be ignorant of the Lord and he will be responsible.

Dads—take an active, godly and manly responsibility for your family!

## 2. TRAINING

A hundred years ago, almost all teachers were men. Today, women easily outnumber men in our school Staff Rooms. The popular perception is that children—especially young children—are to be taught by women. The trouble is, too many Christian families carry this perception into family life.

In 1 Thessalonians 2, Paul says that he dealt with the Thessalonian Christians as a father deals with his own children. He encouraged. He comforted. He urged them to live lives worthy of God. He cheered them on at the touchline.

Those of us who are fathers might like to consider how we too can encourage, comfort and urge our offspring to live holy and godly lives. For many of us, urging comes more naturally than comforting, and encouragement can all too often descend into rebuke. But will we train? Will we instruct? Or will we be swayed by popular culture, and leave it to the ladies.

### 3. MODELLING

We're not talking here about the sort of modelling that David Beckham does for his pocket money. We're talking role models. We all have them—some are good, and some are definitely not good.

Children—especially boys—copy their fathers. Embarrassingly, two of the first electrical devices our toddler learnt to use were the phone and the TV remote control. What does that say about the father he has observed?

This is not to say that children don't copy their mothers, but simply that how fathers speak and behave really matters. Christians seek to be like their heavenly Father, and many people experience a desire to be like (as well as liked by!) their human fathers. But are they being set good examples?

Ephesians 6v1 goes on: 'Children, obey your parents in the Lord, for this is right. "Honour your father and mother"—which is the first commandment with a promise—"that it may go well with you and that you may enjoy long life on the earth."'.

Children must obey their parents. This is the path of godliness. This is the path of blessing (the two always go together!). Obedience is appropriate. Obedience is not an optional

extra. We do our children a great disservice if we do not teach them the important of obedience.

Of course, we need to model obedience—they will quickly pick up whether or not we honour their grandparents. And we need to train them in obedience, because it certainly won't come naturally. And, most of all, we need to take on the responsibility of ensuring that they are obedient—because, while they are children, we (and fathers in particular) are responsible to God for them.

Meanwhile, I shall doubtless continue to exasperate my son. I shall certainly fail in my responsibility to train him and instruct him. Thank goodness that my heavenly Father is full of forgiveness.

*Mark Wallace*

**Dads—take an active, godly and manly responsibility for your family!**

**P.S.** There's an excellent new book coming out soon—**Fatherhood: what it is and what it's for** (by Tony Payne). If you're a Dad, buy it, read it and rejoice in it. If you're a Mum and your children are looking for a Father's Day present or birthday present... what could be better?

(*Available from your local Christian bookshop—or call us on 0845 225 0880 to order a copy.*)

# Lighten up

**KEYPOINT**
Jesus is the Light, so Christians live differently, not in darkness. They can't do it secretly.

Today's passages are:
**Table Talk:** John 12v42-46
**XTB:** John 12v37-50

**TABLE TALK**

Are you ever embarrassed about people knowing that you believe in Jesus? When and why do you feel like that?

**READ**

Many people saw Jesus' miracles, like bringing Lazarus back to life, and they believed in Jesus. But there was a problem... **Read John 12v42-43**

**TALK**

Which of these was true?
**a)** They were scared of the Pharisees.
**b)** They wanted men to praise them.
**c)** They didn't care enough about God.

**READ**

All three were true! These people wanted to believe in Jesus **secretly**, without anyone knowing! BUT what does Jesus say? **Read John 12v44-46**

If people believe in Jesus, who else do they believe in? (v44) (*The one who sent Jesus—that means God.*) Jesus is the Light. So what does that mean for believers? (v46) (*They won't stay in darkness.*)

**THINK**

People live in darkness because they disobey God. But a Christian follows Jesus the Light, so they live differently. You can't do it secretly!

**PRAY**

Ask God to help you to live Jesus' way boldly (not secretly) even if others laugh at you.

### Building up
Do your friends know that you believe in Jesus? Perhaps they laugh about it and make it hard for you. But are you more bothered about what people think? Or about what God thinks of you? Pray together about your answers.

# Serving others

**KEYPOINT**
Jesus washed His disciples feet. We should follow His example and serve others too.

Today's passages are:
**Table Talk:** John 13v4-17
**XTB:** John 13v1-17

**TABLE TALK**

Start today's Table Talk with one of you washing everyone else's feet. How did people feel having their feet washed?

Jesus was having His last meal with His disciples. We've seen that Jesus could do amazing miracles, that showed that He is the **Son of God** and the promised **King**. But at the meal, Jesus did the job of a **servant** by washing His disciples' feet! **Read John 13v4-11**

**READ**

**TALK**

Who didn't want Jesus to wash his feet? (v8) (*Peter*) But Jesus knew that being washed was a picture of something important. What did He tell Peter? (v10) (*A person who's had a bath needs only to wash his feet. His body is clean.*)

**Being washed all over** is a picture of being forgiven for <u>all</u> the wrong things we'll ever do. That happens when we believe in Jesus.

**Having our feet washed** is a picture of saying sorry to God <u>each time</u> we do wrong. And remembering that, through Jesus, we've been forgiven.

**Read John 13v12-17**

What does Jesus tell His followers to do? (v15) (*Follow His example.*)

**THINK**

Like Jesus, we should **serve** others. Write down some names of friends and family. Next to them write how you can **serve** them this week (polish shoes, be nicer to them etc). Don't write down stuff you already do!

**PRAY**

Now ask God to help you do these.

### Building up
Flick back through chapters 9-13 of John's Gospel. What have you learnt about Jesus? What have you learnt about living for Jesus?

## HISTORY HOP

A quick pogo through the history of the Israelites...

### THREE PROMISES

God made three amazing promises to Abraham:

1. **A HUGE family**—the Israelites.

2. **A land of their own**—the land of Israel.

3. **Blessing**—someone from Abraham's family would be God's way of blessing the whole world.

### INTO EGYPT...

The Israelites lived in Egypt for 400 years. They became a HUGE family (over two million!) **just as God had promised**.

But the Egyptians made them into **slaves**!

### INTO ISRAEL...

So God rescued the Israelites from Egypt, and brought them to the land of Israel, **just as He had promised**.

For 400 years the Israelites had a series of leaders called **judges**. After that they had **kings** to lead them.

The best king they ever had was **King David**. David loved God, and helped his people to love God too.

### A WARNING

When David died, his son Solomon became king. God told Solomon what would happen if he and his family loved and obeyed God. He also told Solomon what would happen if he disobeyed God...

**Read 1 Kings 9v4-9** (then return to 'Talk' in the Table Talk section opposite.)

---

# DAY 36
# History = His Story

> **KEYPOINT**
> God warned the Israelites that if they turned away from Him, He'd remove them from the land.

Today's passages are:
**Table Talk:** 1 Kings 9v4-9
**XTB:** 1 Kings 9v4-9

**TABLE TALK**
Read **Notes for Parents** together, for a summary of the history of the Israelites.

**TALK**
If Solomon and his family <u>loved</u> and <u>obeyed</u> God, someone from their family would always rule the Israelites (v4-5). But what would happen if they <u>turned away</u> from God and served pretend gods (idols) instead? (v7) (*God would remove them from the land of Israel.*)

**THINK**
This was a serious warning, which God gave the Israelites many times. It was **God** who had given them the land of Israel to live in. But if they kept turning away from Him, He would <u>remove</u> them from that land.

In the next chunk of 2 Kings we'll see God's warning come true. It's a sad story, as we see the Israelites <u>turned out</u> of their land because they had <u>turned away</u> from God.

But we'll also meet a chap called **Isaiah**. He has some exciting things to say about God's promise that someone from Abraham's family will be **God's way of blessing the whole world!**

**PRAY**
History = <u>His</u> Story. The history of the Israelites teaches us loads about what <u>God</u> is like and how He acts. Ask Him to help you learn more about Him as you read this part of Israel's history.

### Building up
God gave David similar promises and warnings: **read 2 Samuel 7v11b-16**. Although God warns David that He will punish David's son (v14), He also promises that someone from David's family will be King for ever (v13&16). That King is King Jesus!

## DAY 37
# Spot the kings

**KEYPOINT**
God removed the Israelites from their land—as He had warned. God is the Real King.

Today's passages are:
**Table Talk:** 2 Kings 17v16
**XTB:** 2 Kings 17v1-6

**DO** (*You need pencil and paper.*) Draw four crowns on four pieces of paper, and label them as: **Ahaz**, king of Judah; **Hoshea**, king of Israel; **Shalmaneser**, king of Assyria; **So**, king of Egypt.

The Israelites were split into two kingdoms, called **Israel** (in the north) and **Judah** (in the south). *Check out the map on Day 1 to see where they were.*

**READ** Today's sad story is about the kingdom of Israel, and its very <u>last</u> king.
**Read 2 Kings 17v1-6**

**DO** Read the simplified version of the story below. As you do, move the four crowns around to show what happened:

> <u>Hoshea</u> was king of Israel for nine years. Every year, <u>Hoshea</u> paid money to <u>Shalmaneser</u>, the king of Assyria. But one year, <u>Hoshea</u> sent messengers to <u>So</u>, the king of Egypt, asking for help against the Assyrians. When <u>Shalmaneser</u> found out, he had <u>Hoshea</u> thrown into prison. Then <u>Shalmaneser</u> attacked the city of Samaria. He captured the Israelites and sent them away to Assyria.

There are lots of kings in today's story. But there's one missing! Who do you think it is? (*Clue: This King was in charge of <u>everything</u> that happened.*)

**THINK** The king of Assyria was doing what **God** had said would happen. God was in control all the time—**He** is the Real King!

**PRAY** God is far more powerful than any king, president or prime minister! Talk to Him about how that makes you feel.

### Building up
**Read Psalm 145** together—a psalm full of praise for God, our wonderful King!

---

## DAY 38
# Kicked out!

**KEYPOINT**
God had done <u>so much</u> for the Israelites—but still they turned away from Him.

Today's passages are:
**Table Talk:** 2 Kings 17v7-8
**XTB:** 2 Kings 17v7-23

**TABLE TALK** Make a list of things that God has done for you. (*Eg: sent Jesus to die for you, listens to your prayers, given you people to love you and homes to live in...*)

**READ** The Israelites had been kicked out of Israel, and sent away to Assyria. The next few verses tell us **why**...
**Read 2 Kings 17v7-8**

**TALK** Why were the Israelites kicked out of their land? (v7) (*They had sinned against God.*) What had God done for them? (v7) (*Rescued them from Egypt.*) But who did they serve instead of God? (v7) (*Other gods—idols.*)

**THINK** God had done **so much** for the Israelites. He had <u>rescued</u> them from Egypt, brought them to the <u>land</u> He promised, and sent many <u>prophets</u> (messengers) to tell them God's words. But the Israelites turned away from God, and ignored His words. So God punished them by sending them away from their land—just as He had warned them.

**PRAY** What about you? God has done **so much** for you too. Is there anything you need to say sorry to Him for? Think carefully, and then talk to God about it.

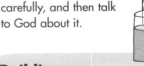

### Building up
The rest of this passage gives details of how the Israelites turned away from God, and carried on living their own way for hundreds of years. They broke God's commands (16), wouldn't listen to His prophets (v14) and in the end were sent into exile as a result (v23).

## DAY 39
# Meet the Samaritans

**KEYPOINT**
Making something else more important than God is sin. And sin must be punished.

Today's passages are:
**Table Talk:** 2 Kings 17v24-28
**XTB:** 2 Kings 17v24-41

**TABLE TALK**

Play **hangman** to guess 'Samaritans'.

Who are the Samaritans? (*A group of people who lived at the time of Jesus and a charity that helps people and a group we'll meet in today's reading!*)

**READ**

When the King of Assyria captured the Israelites and sent them to live in Assyria, he needed to put some other people in their place. They would look after the land and pay him taxes. The people he moved in became known as the **Samaritans** (because they lived in Samaria). **Read 2 Kings 17v24-28**

**TALK**

The people who lived in Samaria didn't worship God. What did He do? (v25) (*He sent lions!*) The king of Assyria heard that God had sent lions because the people in Samaria didn't worship Him. Who did the king send to Samaria? (v27) (*A priest.*) The priest taught the people how to love and serve God. But the people served other gods (idols) as well! (v29-41)

God hates sin. He hates it if people make something else more important than Him. The Samaritans didn't love and serve God—so He sent lions to punish them.

**THINK**

Every time you and I make something else more important than God—or we fail to love and serve God totally—then we are sinning. And that sin must be punished.

**PRAY**

The great news is that God made a way for us to be forgiven. How? (*Jesus died for us.*) God sent Jesus, not a punishment! Are you thankful? Then say so!

### Building up
Find out more about how the Samaritans served both God and idols in **2 Kings 17v32-41**.

---

## DAY 40
# The good Samaritan

**KEYPOINT**
We should love God totally and love others—not to earn a place in heaven, but to please God.

Today's passages are:
**Table Talk:** Luke 10v25-37
**XTB:** Luke 10v25-37

**READ**

Who were the group of people we met yesterday? (*The Samaritans.*) Today we're going to hop into the New Testament to read a story Jesus told about a Samaritan. But first, we'll meet an expert in Old Testament law. He had a question about eternal life... **Read Luke 10v25-28**

**TALK**

The law expert wanted to know how to earn a place in heaven. What was the answer? (*See v27.*) That means:
• Love God totally—all the time.
• Love other people—all the time.
Can you do that? ALL the time??? (*No!*)

**THINK**

The answer is No! So we can't earn our place in heaven. That's why Jesus came and died for us. **He** is the only way we can be forgiven, and one day live with God in heaven.

**DO**

Use **Notes for Parents** on the next page to help you read the story Jesus then told to the law expert.

**THINK**

Who was a neighbour (friend) to the injured man? (*The Samaritan*) Jesus told the law expert to go and do the same. In other words, he had to love his enemies as well as his friends!

**PRAY**

**Love God totally and love other people**. If we are Christians, then this is how we will want to live. Not to earn a place in heaven! But because we want to please God by living His way. Ask God to help you to do this today... and tomorrow... and the day after... and...

### Building up
Look up the Old T laws quoted by the law expert in **Deuteronomy 6v4-7** and **Leviticus 19v18**.

### THE GOOD SAMARITAN [DAY 40]

The law expert had another question for Jesus:

Who is my neighbour?

He wanted to know exactly <u>who</u> he had to love. So Jesus told him a story.

The main characters are:

- A Jewish man (*who gets beaten up*)
- A priest (*chosen to serve God*)
- A Levite (*a helper in God's temple*)
- A Samaritan (*<u>hated</u> by the Jews*)

(*<u>Note</u>: Yesterday's bit of Old Testament history helps us to understand why the Jews hated Samaritans. The Samaritans were living in part of Israel, which was the land God had promised to give to the Israelites as their own. Also, the Samaritans has added the worship of Israel's God to their own religious practices, ending up with a mixed religion.*)

### Read Luke 10v29-37

(*Optional*) Read it again, acting it out.

### BUILDING UP [DAY 41]

**Read 2 Kings 18v4** again. This bronze snake had been provided by God as a means of saving the Israelites when they were bitten by deadly snakes. Anyone who was bitten had to look at the snake and trust God to save them. BUT something provided by God to help His people was now being worshipped <u>instead</u> of God! That's why it had to be destroyed. (*The original story is in Numbers 21v4-9.*)

---

**KEYPOINT**
Hezekiah trusted God. Trusting God isn't just about what we <u>believe</u>, but also what we <u>do</u>.

Today's passages are:
**Table Talk:** 2 Kings 18v1-8
**XTB:** 2 Kings 18v1-8

**TABLE TALK**

Look at the map on Day 1. The people in **Israel** (in the north) had ignored God's warnings and kept sinning against Him. What happened to them? (*They were taken away by the Assyrians.*) Who moved into Israel in their place? (*The Samaritans.*) What kingdom did that leave untouched? (*Judah, in the south.*)

**READ**

In the southern kingdom of **Judah** there was a new king. His name was Hezekiah, and he loved and obeyed God.
**Read 2 Kings 18v1-8**

**TALK**

How old was Hezekiah when he became king? (v2) (*25*) What kind of king was he? (v4&v6) (*He did what was right in God's eyes, like King David had. He was faithful to God and kept all God's commands.*) Hezekiah also destroyed everything that had been used to worship pretend gods (v4).

Verse 5 tells us that Hezekiah **trusted God**. Trusting God isn't just about what we <u>believe</u>. It's also about what we <u>do</u>. Hezekiah did all these things because he trusted God, and believed that obeying God's commands is the best way to live.

**THINK**

What about <u>you</u>? If you trust God you'll want to obey His commands, even when that's hard. Firstly that means:
- Believing in the Lord Jesus.
Then you can live to please God by:
- Always telling the truth. • Loving other people. • Telling others about Jesus. etc

**PRAY**

Ask God to help you trust Him by doing these things.

**Building up**
Read **Notes for Parents** opposite.

## DAY 42
# Who do you trust?

**KEYPOINT**
When people try to knock our confidence in God we must hold on to the truth from the Bible.

Today's passages are:
**Table Talk:** 2 Kings 18v17-25
**XTB:** 2 Kings 18v17-25

**TABLE TALK**

You don't believe all that rubbish in the Bible do you???

Nobody believes in Jesus any more!

How would you feel if you were the girl in the middle of the picture?

**READ**

The king of Assyria, called Sennacherib, attacked Jerusalem. He sent this message to King Hezekiah: 'On what are you basing your trust?' What do you think Hezekiah's answer would be? (*As we saw yesterday, Hezekiah trusted God.*) But Sennacherib tried to <u>knock</u> Hezekiah's trust in God. **Read 2 Kings 18v19-25**

**TALK**

Which verse matches each statement?
• Egypt won't help you.
• God won't help you.
• Your army can't help you.
• It was God who told us to attack you!
(*The answers are v21, v22, v24, v25.*)
Sennacherib was trying to make Hezekiah and the Israelites lose their confidence in God. *Tomorrow we'll see if it worked...*

**THINK**

Do you ever get teased for being a Christian? It can be really tough sometimes. Ask God to help you to hold on the truth from the Bible: that God is the Real King of everything; that God loves you; that He sent Jesus to die for you.

**PRAY**

### Building up
Look again at the cartoon at the top of the page. How could you answer them? (*Eg: tell them <u>why</u> you believe the Bible is true.*)

---

## DAY 43
# Blasphemy

**KEYPOINT**
The king of Assyria said that even God couldn't stop him. That's blasphemy.

Today's passages are:
**Table Talk:** 2 Kings 18v28-36
**XTB:** 2 Kings 18v26-37

**TABLE TALK**

Today's heading is 'blasphemy'. Ask your child which of these they think it means:
**a)** talking too much
**b)** saying things against God
**c)** singing too loudly

**READ**

King Sennacherib of Assyria has sent his messenger to Jerusalem. He is saying stuff against God—that's blasphemy! And the messenger is deliberately speaking in the common language of Hebrew so that the Israelites crowded onto the walls of Jerusalem can all understand him...
**Read 2 Kings 18v28-36**

**TALK**

What did Sennacherib tell the Israelites not to let Hezekiah do? (v30) (*Don't let him persuade them to trust in God.*) Then he told them that no other gods had been able to save their country from the Assyrians. Did Sennacherib think that <u>God</u> could save Jerusalem? (v35) (*No!*)

The message is clear. The king of Assyria thinks he is <u>far</u> more powerful than any god. Not even the LORD can stop him! That's blasphemy! And he's <u>very</u> wrong, as we'll see tomorrow...

**THINK**

Hopefully <u>you'll</u> never say stuff against God the way Sennacherib did! But do you ever use God's name carelessly? Do you ever use God's name (or 'Jesus') as a swear word? Or think wrong things about God? If you do, tell Him you are sorry, and ask Him to help you to change.

**PRAY**

### Building up
God knows all our <u>thoughts</u>, as well as what we <u>say</u>. **Read Psalm 139v1-4**. Ask God to help you to <u>think</u> right things about Him as well as <u>say</u> them.

# DAY 44
## Don't be afraid

**KEYPOINT**
God told Hezekiah not to be afraid. <u>God</u> is the Real King.

Today's passages are:
**Table Talk:** 2 Kings 19v1-7
**XTB:** 2 Kings 19v1-7

**TABLE TALK**

What do you wear at church?
(*You might like to draw your answers.*)

**READ**

Before going to the temple, King Hezekiah <u>ripped</u> his clothes and put on sackcloth! Read the verses to see why.
**Read 2 Kings 19v1-4**

Why did Hezekiah tear his clothes? (*In Bible times, people tore their clothes and wore sackcloth when they were sad or upset. Hezekiah was upset because Sennacherib had threatened Jerusalem and insulted God.*) Hezekiah sent his men to see God's prophet (messenger). What was he called? (v2) (*Isaiah*)

**READ**

Isaiah had a message for Hezekiah. It was a message from God...
**Read 2 Kings 19v5-7**

What three things did God say to Hezekiah? (*Don't be afraid, v6. The king of Assyria will hear a report that will make him return to his own country, v7. He will die there, v7.*)

**THINK**

God told Hezekiah not to be afraid. Why? Because **God** is the Real King. He's <u>far</u> more powerful than the king of Assyria.

**PRAY**

We have the same reason not to be afraid. God is the Real King today too. He is always able to help us, and never lets us down. Talk to Him about any worries you have—and ask Him to help you not to be afraid.

### Building up
The most often repeated command in the Bible is 'Don't be afraid'. It's repeated 366 times. That's one for each day of the year, and one extra in case you have a particularly scary day!

# DAY 45
## The only God

**KEYPOINT**
Hezekiah praised God, told God the problem, and asked God to act to show how great He is.

Today's passages are:
**Table Talk:** 2 Kings 19v14-19
**XTB:** 2 Kings 19v8-19

**TABLE TALK**

Think of some recent letters. Were they nasty (*eg: bills!*) or nice (*eg: telling you about a new baby*).

**READ**

King Hezekiah was sent a very <u>nasty</u> letter. It was from Sennacherib, the king of Assyria. The letter said that <u>no</u> god could stop the Assyrians! When Hezekiah received the letter, he went to the temple to talk to God.
**Read 2 Kings 19v14-19**

**TALK**

Hezekiah's prayer is a great example for us to follow. What did he do first? (v15) (*He praised God, the Real King.*) Then he told God the problem (v16-18). How did Hezekiah end his prayer? (v19) (*He asked God to act in a way that would show how great God is.*)

**PRAY**

Write your own prayer following this same pattern.
1—Praise God.
2—Tell God about any problems.
3—Ask God to act in a way that will show how great He is.

### Building up
Jesus' disciples asked Him to teach them how to pray. Read His answer in **Luke 11v1-4**.

# DAY 46
## A hook in your nose!

**KEYPOINT**
Sennacherib had insulted God. Now God would force him to leave Jerusalem and go home.

Today's passages are:
**Table Talk:** 2 Kings 19v20-28
**XTB:** 2 Kings 19v20-28

**DO**

Find a picture of a horse and rider. Talk about the different parts of a horse's tack (saddle, reins etc). What does a rider use a **bit** for? (*To tell the horse where to go.*)

**READ**

King Hezekiah has been praying in the temple—asking God to save Jerusalem from the Assyrians. Now he gets an answer from God.
**Read 2 Kings 19v20**

**TALK**

Who gives God's answer? (*God's prophet, Isaiah.*) The first part of God's message was to Sennacherib, the king of Assyria. We'll pull out three bits of it:

**Read v22-23a** Who has Sennacherib insulted? (*The LORD.*)

**Read v25** The Assyrians had been destroying cities. But who planned it long ago? (*The LORD.*)

**Read v28** What will the LORD do to Sennacherib? (*Put a hook in his nose, a bit in his mouth and force him to go.*)

**THINK**

A farmer leads a bull by a <u>ring</u> or <u>hook</u> in its nose. A rider uses a <u>bit</u> to tell his horse where to go. In the same way, God would force Sennacherib to leave Jerusalem and return to Assyria. *We'll see how God did that tomorrow.*

**PRAY**

God's enemies (those who hate Christians, the devil) have to do what <u>God</u> wants. Thank God that He's always in control.

### Building up
Read the whole of God's message to Sennacherib in **2 Kings 19v20-28**. Some of the language may be a bit tricky for your child, but it clearly shows how arrogant (and therefore how foolish!) Sennacherib was.

---

# DAY 47
## The hook works

**KEYPOINT**
God always speaks the truth. He is always able to do what He says. Nothing can stop Him.

Today's passages are:
**Table Talk:** 2 Kings 19v35-37
**XTB:** 2 Kings 19v29-37

**TABLE TALK**

God had said:
- 'The king of Assyria will return to his own country and I will cause him to be killed there.' (v7)
- 'I will put my hook in his nose, and my bit in his mouth, and force him to return the way he came.' (v28)

Do you think God's words came true? (*Yes, No, Not sure.*) <u>Why</u> do you think that?

**READ**

Read the passage to find out.
**Read 2 Kings 19v35-37**

**TALK**

Who went to the Assyrian camp? (v35) (*The angel of the LORD.*) How many Assyrians were killed? (v35) (*185,000*) God had said the king of Assyria would return home (to Assyria, and its capital city Nineveh). Did he? (v36) (*Yes*) God had said the king of Assyria would be killed in Assyria. Was he? (v37) (*Yes*)

**THINK**

God's words <u>always</u> come true. Why? (*Ask your child their reasons. Make sure they understand the following three:*
**1**—*God always speaks the <u>truth</u>.*
**2**—*God is always <u>able</u> to do what He says.*
**3**—*Nothing and no one can <u>stop</u> God's plans!*)

**PRAY**

Thank and praise God for these things.

### Building up
God **rescued** His people just as He promised. Can you think of other examples of God rescuing His people? (*Eg: rescuing the Israelites from Egypt, sending His Son to rescue us from our sins...*)

# DAY 48 Surprising shadow sign

**KEYPOINT**
God heard Hezekiah's prayer and healed him.

Today's passages are:
**Table Talk:** 2 Kings 20v1-11
**XTB:** 2 Kings 20v1-11

**TABLE TALK**

Make a list of anyone you know who is ill. Keep the list for later.

**READ**

King Hezekiah became ill. <u>Very</u> ill. In fact, he was going to die!
**Read 2 Kings 20v1-3**

What did Hezekiah do? (*v2—He prayed; v3—He wept.*)

**THINK**

When you're ill, or upset, do you pray about it? You can talk to God about <u>anything</u>—and it's OK to show Him how upset you are, too!

**READ**

God heard Hezekiah's prayer, and sent Isaiah back with another message...
**Read 2 Kings 20v4-7**

**TALK**

What was God's message? (v5) (*'I have heard your prayer and seen your tears. I will heal you.'*) Instead of dying, how much longer was Hezekiah going to live? (v6) (*Another 15 years.*)

**READ**

That was great news! But Hezekiah wanted a **sign** that it would really happen just as God said...
**Read 2 Kings 20v8-11**

Nobody's quite sure what this sign was. It may have been a special staircase that used a shadow to tell the time (a bit like a sundial). Whatever it was, we **do** know that God generously gave Hezekiah the sign he asked for.

**PRAY**

Read **Notes for Parents** about praying for people who are ill. Then pray for the people on your list.

**Building up**
See **Notes for Parents** for Building Up.

## PRAYING FOR PEOPLE

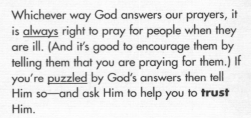

Praying for people who are ill can feel a bit puzzling. Sometimes God heals them quickly (like Hezekiah). Sometimes He heals them slowly, and uses doctors and nurses to make them better. And sometimes they may not get better at all. That doesn't mean God hasn't heard our prayers! But He may have a good reason for saying No.

Whichever way God answers our prayers, it is <u>always</u> right to pray for people when they are ill. (And it's good to encourage them by telling them that you are praying for them.) If you're **puzzled** by God's answers then tell Him so—and ask Him to help you to **trust** Him.

Do you remember reading about the blind man, and Jesus' friend Lazarus, in John's Gospel? The Bible tells us that these men were ill so that <u>God's work</u> could be seen in their lives.

Check out **John 9v3** and **John 11v4 & v14-15**.

**Building up**
We don't need to use lots of words when we pray. God already knows what we need. Read Jesus' teaching about this in **Matthew 6v7-8**.

# DAY 49 Visitors from Babylon

**KEYPOINT**
Hezekiah showed everything to the Babylonians. One day it would all go to Babylon!

Today's passages are:
**Table Talk:** 2 Kings 20v12-19
**XTB:** 2 Kings 20v12-21

**TABLE TALK**

**Flashback:** The Israelites were split into two kingdoms. What were they called? (*Israel and Judah—see map on Day 1.*) God had <u>warned</u> the people of **Israel** that if they kept sinning, they'd be taken away from their land. What happened? (*They ignored God's warnings, so they were carried away by the Assyrians.*)

**READ**

Hezekiah was the king of **Judah**. Was he a good or bad king? (*Good, because he loved and obeyed God.*) BUT God had made the same <u>warning</u> to the people of Judah. If they turned away from God, they would be turned out of their country. **Read 2 Kings 20v12-19**

**TALK**

Where were the messengers from? (v12) (*Babylon*) What did Hezekiah show them? (v15) (*Everything!*) Then Isaiah turned up with a message from God. What was God's message? (v17) (*The time will come when <u>everything</u> in the palace will be carried off to Babylon.*)

**THINK**

It wouldn't happen while Hezekiah was alive—but it <u>would</u> happen. The people of Judah would be taken away, just like the people of Israel. *More about that when we return to 2 Kings on Day 56.*

**PRAY**

Hezekiah had been a good king, like King David. But he wasn't perfect! God's <u>perfect</u> King, also from David's family, would be born 700 years later. Who is He? (*Jesus*) Thank God for sending King Jesus to be our perfect King.

## Building up
We can also read about Hezekiah in the book of Isaiah. Read a song of praise written by Hezekiah in **Isaiah 38v9-20**.

---

# DAY 50 Wholly holy

**KEYPOINT**
Isaiah saw a vision of God as King of the universe, holy, perfect and pure.

Today's passages are:
**Table Talk:** Isaiah 6v1-4
**XTB:** Isaiah 6v1-4

**TABLE TALK**

Ask your child what job they'd like to do when they grow up. Tell them any jobs you have had, and how you got them.

**READ**

We're going to jump out of **2 Kings** for a few days to find out how the prophet **Isaiah** got his job as God's messenger. **Read Isaiah 6v1-4**

**TALK**

Isaiah saw a great King, sitting on a throne. But it wasn't King Uzziah! Who was the King? (v1) (*The LORD*) How is God described? (v1) (*Seated on a throne. High and exalted. His robe filled the temple.*) Wow! God is the King of the whole universe! No one is higher or more powerful than Him!

The throne was surrounded by **seraphs**. These amazing creatures were like fiery angels. They <u>worshipped</u> God. What were they saying? (v3) (*Holy, holy, holy is the Lord Almighty! The whole earth is full of His glory.*) Wow! That means that God is totally perfect and pure! He made the whole earth, and it shows how great and wonderful He is!

**DO**

Copy the seraph's words from v3 onto a large sheet of paper. You could try drawing some seraphs round it!

**PRAY**

Pray together, praising God for being King of the universe, perfect and pure.

## Building up
There is another picture of God being praised by these amazing creatures in the last book in the Bible. **Read Revelation 4v6-11**.

# DAY 51
## Unclean lips

**KEYPOINT**
Isaiah was 'unclean' and didn't deserve to be with God. But God made him clean again.

Today's passages are:
**Table Talk:** Isaiah 6v5-7
**XTB:** Isaiah 6v5-7

**TABLE TALK**

Recap: Who did Isaiah see in yesterday's reading? (*God*) What did He look like? (*A King on a throne, surrounded by fiery angels.*) What do you think Isaiah thought and felt when he saw God?

Read the passage to find out.
**Read Isaiah 6v5**

What did Isaiah say? (v5) (*'Woe to me! I am a man of unclean lips. My eyes have seen the King, the LORD Almighty.'*)

**THINK**

Isaiah didn't have a muddy face (!), so what does 'unclean lips' mean? (*Isaiah knew he was sinful. Even his lips spoke sinful words.*)

**READ**

God is holy, perfect and pure. Isaiah knew he didn't deserve to be with God. In fact, he deserved to die! But God did something wonderful for Isaiah...
**Read Isaiah 6v6-7**

**TALK**

What did the seraph do? (*Flew to Isaiah with a burning coal from the altar and touched Isaiah's lips with it.*) What happened as a result? (*Isaiah's guilt was taken away and his sins forgiven.*)

**THINK**

God made Isaiah clean again! His sins were forgiven. Who has made it possible for *our* sins to be forgiven? (*Jesus*) More about that on Day 55.

**PRAY**

Thank God for sending Jesus so that we can be made clean and have our sins forgiven.

### Building up
'Unclean' is a word the Bible uses to describe the result of sin. It separates us from our perfect, pure God. But Jesus was 'clean'. He never sinned. His death makes it possible for us to be made 'clean' too—**1 Peter 3v18a**.

# DAY 52
## Send me

**KEYPOINT**
Isaiah offered to serve God as His messenger. Have you told God you want to serve Him?

Today's passages are:
**Table Talk:** Isaiah 6v8-10
**XTB:** Isaiah 6v8-13

**TABLE TALK**

Who do you know who works 'full-time' for God? (*Eg: vicar or minister, church youth worker, missionary...*)

**READ**

Isaiah was about to be given a full-time job as God's messenger...
**Read Isaiah 6v8-10**

**TALK**

What was God's question? (v8) (*'Whom shall I send'?'*) How did Isaiah answer? (v8) (*'Send me!'*) Isaiah had volunteered to be God's messenger—but what was God's hard message? (v9) (*Be hearing but never understanding.*) God's people had turned away from Him. So now they wouldn't <u>understand</u> God's message to them.

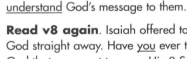

**Read v8 again**. Isaiah offered to serve God straight away. Have <u>you</u> ever told God that you want to serve Him? Serving God isn't just for 'full-timers', like the people you thought about earlier. It isn't just for adults either!!! If <u>you</u> want to serve God with your life, then ask Him to show you how He wants you to do that.

**THINK**

**PRAY**

Pray together about this now.

### Building up
The land God had given to His people would be ruined. But there was still a <u>hint</u> of a hope to come... **Read Isaiah 6v11-13**

What will be left? (v13) (*A stump.*) New trees can grow from bare stumps. In the same way, there was still a <u>hope</u> for the people of Judah. Out of the very few who accepted God, His people would grow again. And one of them would be the perfect King they were waiting for!

# DAY 53
## To us a child is born

**KEYPOINT**
Jesus is the 'great light'. He is the mighty and everlasting King Isaiah spoke about.

Today's passages are:
**Table Talk:** Isaiah 9v1-2 & 6-7
**XTB:** Isaiah 9v1-7

**TABLE TALK** Have you been to a Christmas Carol Service? What was it like? Today's passage is often read at Carol Services.

Isaiah had a hard message for the Israelites. But there were some fantastic clues about the perfect King whom God had promised to send. **Read Isaiah 9v1-2**

**READ**

**TALK** What have the people walking in darkness seen? (v2) (*A great light.*) Where would this great light be seen? (v1) (*Galilee, in the area of Zebulun and Naphtali.*) This 'great light' is a person, who grew up in Nazareth, a town in Galilee. Who is this 'great light'? (*Jesus*)

**READ** Isaiah went on to say that God's people would have peace when their perfect King came. **Read Isaiah 9v6-7**

**TALK** Find four fantastic names for Jesus (v6). (*Wonderful Counsellor, Mighty God, Everlasting Father, Prince of Peace.*) These names remind us that Jesus shows us the best way to live, and brings us peace with God. Jesus is God! He is mighty and everlasting!

How long will Jesus be King? (v7) (*For ever!*)

**PRAY** **Wow!** Jesus is our perfect King! He is still alive today—and will rule as King for ever! Thank, praise and obey Him now.

### Building up
In Matthew's book about Jesus, he uses these words from Isaiah to show that Jesus is the promised King. **Read Matthew 4v12-17.**

---

# DAY 54
## Suffering servant

**KEYPOINT**
Jesus, our perfect King, came as a suffering servant, to rescue us from our sins.

Today's passages are:
**Table Talk:** Isaiah 53v3
**XTB:** Isaiah 53v3

**TABLE TALK** Make a list of some of the ways Isaiah has described Jesus: Great Light, Wonderful Counsellor, Mighty God, Prince of Peace. Now play **hangman** to discover another way that Isaiah described Jesus. (*'Suffering Servant'*)

**READ** Jesus is fantastic! You would expect everyone to be thrilled when this perfect King arrived. But they weren't! **Isaiah 52v13–53v12** was written hundreds of years before Jesus was born. But it describes how people would hate Jesus and turn their backs on Him, even though he had come as their perfect King. **Read Isaiah 53v3**

**THINK** Think about what those words mean:
Despised: People looked down on Jesus.
Rejected: People turned away from Jesus.
Suffering: Jesus died a horrible, painful death.

WHY did Jesus go through all of this? (*Because He came to die, to rescue us from our sins.*)

**PRAY** Thank Jesus for being willing to be despised and rejected, and to suffer so much, to be our Rescuer and King.

### Building up
Read the whole 'Suffering Servant' section in **Isaiah 52v13–53v12** looking out for other clues that point to Jesus. *We'll look at v4-6 in more detail tomorrow.*

# DAY 55
# We're all like sheep...

**KEYPOINT**
We're like sheep who've got lost—we've gone our own way instead of God's way.

Today's passages are:
**Table Talk:** Isaiah 53v4-6
**XTB:** Isaiah 53v4-6

Ahem! The book of Isaiah has some tricky terms in it. Just in case—here are a few you might meet today.

**Sins/Infirmities/Transgressions/Iniquities**
All of these words are used for our **sin**, when we do what <u>we</u> want instead of what <u>God</u> wants.

**Stricken/Smitten/Afflicted**
These words mean that Jesus was made to <u>suffer</u>.

As you read today's verses, remember that Jesus <u>chose</u> to suffer, so that He could be our Rescuer. **Read Isaiah 53v4-6**

What are we all like? (v6) (*Sheep who have wandered off and got lost.*) Which was have we all gone? (v6) (*Our own way.*) We've gone our <u>own</u> way, instead of <u>God's</u> way. That's called **sin**—and must be punished. But what has God done with our punishment? (v6) (*God has made the punishment we deserve fall on Jesus.*)

Re-read *'The lost sheep'* in **Notes for Parents** on **Day 21**.

Have you put your trust in Jesus to rescue you?

No?—then ask Him to.
Yes?—then thank Him right now!

### Building up
We are 'justified' by Jesus' death. '<u>Justified</u>' means '<u>just as if I'd</u> never sinned'. As a result, we have peace with God and will one day live with Him in heaven. **Read Romans 4v25–5v1**.

# DAYS 56–65
# Notes for Parents

## HISTORY HOP (AGAIN!)

Welcome back to the book of **2 Kings**. Here's a quick reminder of what's happened so far to the kingdoms of Israel and Judah.

### ISRAEL
- God **warned** them that they must love and obey Him.
- They **ignored** God's warnings.
- So they were **captured** by the Assyrians and taken away from their country.

### JUDAH
- God **warned** them that they must love and obey Him.
- IF they **ignored** God's warnings, they would be **captured** by their enemies (as Israel were) and taken away from their country.

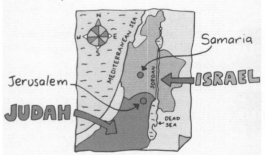

Last time, we met **King Hezekiah**, who was the <u>best</u> king Judah ever had.

But his son **Manasseh** was an <u>evil</u> king, who made God very angry (2 Kings 21v6).

And Hezekiah's grandson **Amon** was also an <u>evil</u> king, just like Manasseh.

Because Manasseh and Amon <u>ignored</u> God's warnings, God did what He said He would. He allowed their enemies to <u>capture</u> the people of Judah.

# DAY 56
# A very young king

**KEYPOINT**
Josiah chose to love God and obey Him. Young or old, we can make that choice too.

Today's passages are:
**Table Talk:** 2 Kings 22v1-2
**XTB:** 2 Kings 22v1-2

**TABLE TALK**

Start today's Table Talk by reading **Notes for Parents** together.

**READ**

In the next few days we'll read the sad story of Judah being attacked and captured. But they had one more good king first... **Read 2 Kings 22v1-2**

**TALK**

Who was the new king? (v1) (*Josiah*) How old was he when he became king? (v1) (*Eight years old.*) What kind of king was Josiah? (v2) (*A good king like his ancestor David.*)

Ask your child what kind of things they hope to do when they're older. (*Eg: get a job, get married, drive a car, be a pop star or sports star, have children...*)

**THINK**

As we grow up, we have lots of choices to make—such as what job to do, or whether to get married. But you don't have to wait until you're older to make the important choice that Josiah made! Josiah chose to **love** God and **obey** Him. And Josiah lived that way all his life.

**PRAY**

What about you? How do you want to live you life? (*Whatever age you are!*) Talk about this, then pray together about your answers.

## Building up
Josiah's grandfather, Manasseh, had also been young when he became king. But he chose to live an evil life, instead of loving and obeying God. **Read 2 Kings 21v1-6**.

# DAY 57
# A book is found

**KEYPOINT**
Josiah knew God's words were hugely important.

Today's passages are:
**Table Talk:** 2 Kings 22v10-13
**XTB:** 2 Kings 22v3-13

**TABLE TALK**

**Recap:** Which king did we meet yesterday? (*Josiah*) What kind of king was he? (*A good king, who loved God.*)

Yesterday, we also saw that God had warned the people of Judah to love and obey Him. If they didn't, God would allow them to be captured by their enemies. **We know** that God was going to carry out His warning soon.
But **Josiah** didn't know that—yet!

**READ**

In today's reading, good King Josiah is now 26 years old. He sent Shaphan, his secretary (assistant), to see how the temple repairs were getting on. Shaphan came back with some news...
**Read 2 Kings 22v10-13**

**TALK**

What did Shaphan have? (v10) (*A book*) This book, written on a scroll, had been found in the temple (v8). It was probably part of the Old Testament. What did Josiah do when he heard God's words in the book? (v11) (*He tore his robes.*) Why was Josiah so upset? (v13) (*He knew God was angry because the people hadn't obeyed God's words in the book.*)

Josiah's father and grandfather hadn't cared about God's words. But Josiah was very different. He knew that God's words were hugely important. And he knew that God would do what He had warned.

**THINK**

How do you react to God's words in the Bible? Do you rush through Table Talk as fast as you can? Do you ask God to speak to you through His Word?

**PRAY**

Talk to God about your answers.

## Building up
Learn **Psalm 119v105** together.

**KEYPOINT**
Judgement and grace are two sides of God's character. They both have to be there.

Today's passages are:
**Table Talk:** 2 Kings 22v14-20
**XTB:** 2 Kings 22v14-20

**DO**

Make a large coin out of a circle of paper or card. Fill in the two sides of the coin as shown in **Notes for Parents**.

**READ**

Josiah tore his robes in sorrow when he heard God's words read to him from the book that had been found in the temple. He sent his men to see a prophetess (God's messenger) called **Huldah** to find out more...
**Read 2 Kings 22v14-20**

**TALK**

These verses show us two sides of God's character. They seem quite different, but <u>both</u> have to be there—like the two sides of the same coin...

**Judgement** (*Show the judgement side of the coin.*) How was God going to punish His people? (v16) (*By bringing disaster on the land of Judah and its people.*) God was going to punish the people of Judah for turning away from Him.

**Grace** (*Show the grace side of the coin.*) How would God show grace (huge kindness) to Josiah? (v20) (*He promised not to punish the people while Josiah was alive.*)

**THINK**

Both sides of God's character are still there today. Think of some ways that God has shown His **grace** to you. (*eg: answering your prayers, sending Jesus to save you from your sins...*)

**PRAY**

Thank God for these things now.

### Building up
See **Notes for Parents** for today's *Building Up* suggestion.

## GOD'S CHARACTER
God is a God of both judgement and grace. He is both at the same time—like the two sides of one coin...

*Make your own coin, as shown:*

### GRACE
**Grace** is God's HUGE kindness to people who don't deserve it.

### JUDGEMENT
**Judgement** means that God makes sure that sin is punished.

### Building up
**Read Malachi 3v6**. God <u>never</u> changes, so all the things you've read about Him are still true today. Write out the first part of this verse, and display it next to the coin you made today.

## DAY 59
# Party time

**KEYPOINT**
Josiah and his people cleaned up their lives and the temple—then celebrated Passover.

Today's passages are:
**Table Talk:** 2 Kings 23v1-3 & 21-23
**XTB:** 2 Kings 23v1-12

**TABLE TALK**

My mum has just had a party. She spent ages cleaning up first! What was the last party you went to?

**READ**

2 Kings 23 tells us of some cleaning up King Josiah did, before a fantastic party...
**Read 2 Kings 23v1-3**

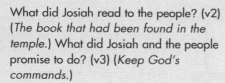
**TALK**

What did Josiah read to the people? (v2) (*The book that had been found in the temple.*) What did Josiah and the people promise to do? (v3) (*Keep God's commands.*)

As well as making this promise, Josiah made sure that anything used to worship pretend gods (idols) was cleared out of the temple (v4-7). And the places used to worship idols were destroyed (v8-20).

**READ**

Then it was party time!
**Read 2 Kings 23v21-23**

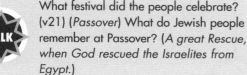
**TALK**

What festival did the people celebrate? (v21) (*Passover*) What do Jewish people remember at Passover? (*A great Rescue, when God rescued the Israelites from Egypt.*)

**PRAY**

Can you be like Josiah and his people?
**First:** Have a 'clean up' by saying sorry to God for the times you've let Him down this week. Ask Him to help you to change.

**THINK**

**Next:** Think of a way to celebrate an even greater Rescue—the fact that Jesus has rescued you from your sins. Could you sing a song thanking God? Bake a 'thank you' cake? Have a party? ...

### Building up
Read about the first ever Passover meal in
**Exodus 12v1-14**.

## DAY 60
# God's judgement

**KEYPOINT**
God brought judgement on the people of Judah—just as He said He would.

Today's passages are:
**Table Talk:** 2 Kings 24v18-20
**XTB:** 2 Kings 23v25–24v20

**DO**

**Quick Quiz** (about Josiah):
• How old was Josiah when he became king? (*8 years old*)
• What was found while Josiah was having the temple repaired? (*A book*)
• What did Josiah do when he heard the words of the book? (*Tore his clothes.*)
• How did Josiah obey God's words in the book? (*He and his people promised to keep God's commands; He cleaned up the temple and destroyed the places where pretend gods were worshipped; He celebrated Passover.*)

**DO**

Josiah was a good king. But read the picture story in **Notes for Parents** on the next page to see what happened after Josiah died.

**READ**

After Nebuchadnezzar had taken most of the people back to Babylon, he made Zedekiah the new king of Jerusalem...
**Read 2 Kings 24v18-20**

**TALK**

What kind of king was Zedekiah? (v19) (*An evil king.*) Why did all these things happen to Judah and Jerusalem? (v20) (*Because God was angry with them.*)

Look again at the two-sided coin you made on Day 58. There are two sides to God's character—judgement and grace. Today we've seen God's **judgement**—just as He said it would happen. Does God's judgement scare you? It should!
**But** if you've put your trust in Jesus then He has rescued you, and you have nothing to be scared of. That's **grace**!

**PRAY**

Talk to God about this now.

### Building up
The Bible makes it very clear that God was behind the disaster that fell on Judah: **read 2 Kings 24v2-4 & 13**.

## DAY 60
# Notes for Parents

## GOD'S JUDGEMENT

There was never a king like Josiah.

He obeyed God with all his heart, soul and strength. (2 Kings 23v25)

But God was still angry with the people of Judah.

I will reject Judah and Jerusalem!

After Josiah died, his son Jehoahaz became king.

But he was an evil king!

The next king was called Jehoiakim.

He was an evil king too!

Jehoiakim was followed by Jehoiachin!

He was another evil king!

Then Nebuchadnezzar, king of Babylon, captured Jerusalem.

—just as God had said.

Nebuchadnezzar removed all the treasures from the temple.

—just as God had said.

Nebuchadnezzar also took the king, his army and most of the people back to Babylon.

—just as God had said.

Taken from 2 Kings 23v25–24v17.

### Building up
Do you remember Hezekiah showing all his riches to some messengers from Babylon? Now everything had gone to Babylon—just as God had told Hezekiah it would! **Read 2 Kings 20v14-18.**

---

## DAY 61
# God is with us

**KEYPOINT**
God's temple was burned down, as a sign that God was <u>not</u> with His people any more.

Today's passages are:
**Table Talk:** 2 Kings 25v8-12
**XTB:** 2 Kings 25v1-30

**TABLE TALK**

The **temple** in Jerusalem was a magnificent building, beautifully decorated and full of gold. But that's <u>not</u> why it was special. The temple was special because it reminded the Israelites of something very important. Today's heading shows what that was. (*The temple reminded God's people that* **He** *was with them.*)

**READ**

BUT the king of Jerusalem (Zedekiah) rebelled against the king of Babylon (Nebuchadnezzar). So Nebuchadnezzar sent his army to Jerusalem...
**Read 2 Kings 25v8-12**

**TALK**

What happened to the temple? (v9) (*It was burned down.*) When God's temple was burned down, it was a sign that God was <u>not</u> with His people any more. He had rejected them—just as He had warned them. The people were taken away to exile (to live in Babylon).

**THINK**

What a sad end! But it's not quite the end of 2 Kings. 37 years later, King Jehoiachin (a captive in Babylon) was freed from prison (v27-30). Why? Because God had promised <u>not</u> to wipe out the family line of King David. (2 Sam 7v16) One day, someone from that family would be born as God's perfect King. And one of His names would be 'Immanuel', which means 'God with us'!

**PRAY**

Who is this perfect King? (*Jesus*) Thank God for keeping His promise to send our perfect King.

### Building up
See **Notes for Parents** for today's *Building Up.*

# DAY 62
# A letter from God

**KEYPOINT**
God punished His people—but He didn't forget them! He never forgets us either.

Today's passages are:
**Table Talk:** Jeremiah 29v4-7 & v10
**XTB:** Jeremiah 29v1-10

**Recap:** Who captured Jerusalem and its people? (*King Nebuchadnezzar*) Where were the Israelites taken? (*To Babylon*)

After the Israelites were taken to Babylon, they were sent a <u>letter</u>. It was written by one of God's prophets (messengers) called **Jeremiah**. Although it was Jeremiah who <u>wrote</u> the letter, the message was from **God**... **Read Jeremiah 29v4-7**

<u>Who</u> had taken the people away from their country? (It's called exile.) Was it God? Or Nebuchadnezzar? (*Both. It was **God** who sent the people away, and He used <u>Nebuchadnezzar</u> to do it.*) What were the people to do now? (v5-7) (*Build houses, plant gardens, marry, have children, pray for the city they lived in.*)

It was God who took His people into exile. Now they had to accept it, and settle down there. But God also made a promise! **Read Jeremiah 29v10**

God promised to bring His people back home. How long would they have to wait? (v10) (*70 years*)

The Israelites <u>deserved</u> to be in exile. It was their punishment for turning away from God. But God didn't **forget** His people. He got Jeremiah to write them a letter. And He gave them a great promise.

God never forgets <u>you</u> either! The whole Bible is like a huge letter from God to you. What do you like best about God's letter, the Bible? Thank Him for it now.

**PRAY**

### Building up
Read how Jeremiah got his job as one of God's prophets in **Jeremiah 1v4-10**.

---

# DAY 63 God's generous promise

**KEYPOINT**
God made generous promises to the Israelites. God loves to be generous.

Today's passages are:
**Table Talk:** Jeremiah 29v10-14
**XTB:** Jeremiah 29v10-14

We're reading a letter written to the Israelites who were living in Babylon. Who <u>wrote</u> the letter? (*Jeremiah*) Who was it really from? (*God*) What had God promised them? (*To bring them home again after 70 years.*)

Now God has some other wonderful things to say to the Israelites...
**Read Jeremiah 29v10-14**

What are God's plans for His people? (v11) (*Good plans, to give them hope and a future.*) What will happen when they call on God? (v12) (*He will listen to them.*) What will happen when they seek God? (v13) (*They will find Him.*)

The Israelites didn't deserve such <u>good</u> things from God—but He generously promised them anyway. What do we call God's HUGE kindness to people who don't deserve it? (*Grace*)

**PRAY**

(*You need pencil and paper.*) God loves to be generous! He gives us so many good things. Jot some down on some paper—then write a huge '**THANK YOU**' underneath. (*If you're stuck for ideas, there are some in Building Up below.*)

### Building up
God's **grace** to us includes:

He looks after the world we live in; He gives us the food, water and air we need to live; He listens to our prayers; He gives us homes to live in and people to take care of us; He sent His own Son to rescue us; and much, much more...

# DAY 64
# Hide and seek

Today's passages are:
**Table Talk** : Jeremiah 29v12-13
**XTB** : Jeremiah 29v12-13

**Either:** Play a quick game
of 'Hide and Seek'
**or:** Talk about hiding
places you have used.
Did you ever choose such a good hiding
place that you couldn't be found???

In yesterday,s reading, God told His
people to **seek** Him. But God isn't
hiding—He **wants** to be found!!!
**Read Jeremiah 29v12-13**

How does God want us to seek Him?
(v13) (*With all our heart.*)

'Seeking' God doesn't mean looking for
Him with a telescope! How can _you_ seek
and find God? (*Discuss your ideas.*)

The best way to find God is by reading
His book to us, the Bible, and then
praying about what we read. It also helps
to meet with other Christians so that we
can help each other to get to know God
better. List three ways that you can seek
God this week:

1 _____

2 _____

3 _____

Ask God to help you to find Him and get
to know Him better as you do these.

## Building up
**Read Psalm 119v9-16**. (*Note: Most
Bible versions have 'I seek you with all my
heart' in v10. A few versions rephrase this
as 'With all my heart I try to serve you.'.*)

# DAY 65
# Getting to know God

Today's passages are:
**Table Talk** : John 14v6-11
**XTB** : John 14v6-11

 **TABLE TALK**

(*You need pencil and paper.*) Write
down some words to describe what **Jesus**
is like (*eg: loving*).

**READ**

Yesterday we saw that God wants us to
find Him. Today we're jumping into John's
Gospel to see what **Jesus** said about how
we can find and know God. In these
verses, Jesus calls God 'the Father'...
**Read John 14v6-11**

Anyone who has
seen me has
seen the Father.

 **TALK**

What did Philip want Jesus to do? (v8)
(*Show them 'the Father'—God.*) How did
Jesus answer Philip? Who do we look at if
we want to see God the Father? (v9) (*We
look at Jesus.*)

 **THINK**

**Wow!** If we want to see what _God_ is
like, we can look at _Jesus_. Look again at
the list of words you wrote to describe
Jesus. These words also show us what
God, our perfect Father, is like.

 **PRAY**

Use those words in a prayer to thank God
for being like this. Now ask God to help
you to get to know Him better and better
as you learn more about Jesus together.

## Building up
Flick back through this issue of Table Talk to
remind yourselves of some of the things you've
read in God's Word, the Bible. Thank Him for the
things He has been teaching you.

# Extra Readings

## WHY ARE THERE EXTRA READINGS?

**Table Talk** and **XTB** both come out every three months. The main Bible reading pages contain material for 65 days. That's enough to use them Monday to Friday for three months.

Many families find that their routine is different at weekends from during the week. Some find that regular Bible reading fits in well on school days, but not at weekends. Others encourage their children to read the Bible for themselves during the week, then explore the Bible together as a family at weekends, when there's more time to do the activities together.

The important thing is to help your children get into the habit of reading the Bible for themselves—and that they see that regular

Bible reading is important for **you** as well.

If you **are** able to read the Bible with your children every day, that's great! The extra readings on the next page will augment the main **Table Talk** pages so that you have enough material to cover the full three months.

You could:

- Read **Table Talk** every day for 65 days, then use the extra readings for the rest of the third month.

- Read **Table Talk** on weekdays. Use the extra readings at weekends.

- Use any other combination that works for your family.

## NAMES AND TITLES FOR JESUS

As we saw on Day 53, the prophet Isaiah knew some of the names for Jesus hundreds of years <u>before</u> Jesus was born! In these extra readings we're going to discover many more...

### Jesus

*These extra readings come from many different books in the Bible. Each one looks at a name or title for Jesus, and explains what that name means.*

There are 26 Bible readings on the next three pages. Part of each verse has been printed for you—but with a word missing. Fill in the missing words as you read the verses. Then see if you can find them all in the wordsearch.

**Note:** Some are written backwards—or diagonally!!

| B | E | A | R | E | S | U | R | R | E | C | T | I | O | N |
|---|---|---|---|---|---|---|---|---|---|---|---|---|---|---|
| E | R | D | E | V | A | S | W | A | Y | L | M | A | S | H |
| G | R | E | E | N | V | O | B | E | L | I | E | V | E | A |
| I | I | S | A | D | I | C | X | T | B | G | O | O | R | T |
| N | S | T | A | R | O | H | F | A | T | H | E | R | V | I |
| N | B | M | A | L | U | R | E | D | B | T | S | T | E | M |
| I | X | T | B | P | R | I | N | C | E | L | A | S | A | M |
| N | A | M | E | R | U | S | H | V | A | N | V | R | O | A |
| G | A | T | D | G | A | T | E | I | N | T | E | I | L | N |
| X | T | F | O | U | N | D | U | N | X | T | B | F | S | U |
| B | W | H | O | B | I | B | L | E | Y | A | D | O | T | E |
| Y | T | H | G | I | M | W | O | N | D | E | R | F | U | L |

# Extra Readings

**1** ☐ **Read Matthew 1v18-21**

The name **Jesus** means 'God Saves'. It tells us <u>who</u> Jesus is: He is **God**; and what Jesus <u>does</u>: He **saves** us from our sins.
'You are to give Him the name Jesus, because He will s _ _ _ His people from their sins.' (v21)

**2** ☐ **Read Matthew 1v22-25**

Jesus was also given the name **Immanuel** (sometimes written as 'Emmanuel'). This name means 'God with us'.
'He will be called
I _ _ _ _ _ _ _ .' (v23)

**3** ☐ **Read Luke 2v11-14**

The angels told the shepherds that Jesus, their **Saviour** (Rescuer), had been born.
'This very day in David's town your
S _ _ _ _ _ _ was born—Christ the Lord!' (v11)

**4** ☐ **Read Mark 1v1**

Jesus is often called **Jesus Christ**. This isn't His surname! 'Christ' is a Greek name meaning 'God's chosen King'.
'The beginning of the gospel (good news) about Jesus C _ _ _ _ _ _ , the Son of God.' (v1)

**5** ☐ **Read John 1v40-42**

**Christ** is a Greek name. The same name in the Hebrew language is **Messiah**.
'We have f _ _ _ _ the Messiah.' (v41)

**6** ☐ **Read John 20v30-31**

Jesus was a human being, like you and me. But He is also God! The Bible often calls Jesus **'the Son of God'**.
'These have been written in order that you may b _ _ _ _ _ _ that Jesus is the Christ, the Son of God.' (v31)

**7** ☐ **Read Luke 19v1-10**

Jesus sometimes called Himself the **'Son of Man'**. He said that He came to look for and rescue lost people.
'The Son of Man came to seek and to s _ _ _ the lost.' (v10)

**8** ☐ **Read Matthew 21v1-9**

God had promised that someone from King David's family would be King for ever. Jesus was that promised **'Son of David'**.
'Hosanna to the Son of David! Blessed is He who comes in the n _ _ _ of the Lord!' (v9)

**9** ☐ **Read Matthew 21v10-11**

Jesus was born in Bethlehem, but He grew up in the town of Nazareth. So He was sometimes called **'Jesus of Nazareth'**.
' "W _ _ is this?" the people asked.' (v10)

**10** ☐ **Read John 6v32-35**

There are seven 'I AM' sayings in John's Gospel, when Jesus said "I am...". In the first one, Jesus says He is like bread that gives eternal life.
'I am the b _ _ _ _ of life.' (v35)

# Extra Readings

**11 ☐ Read John 8v12**

The devil wants people to be lost in darkness—without God. But Jesus brings light!
'I am the **L** _ _ _ _ of the world.' (v12)

**12 ☐ Read John 10v7-10**

Jesus is like a gate or door. He is the only way to be rescued from our sins and live for ever in heaven.
'I am the **g** _ _ _ . Whoever enters by me will be saved.' (v9)

**13 ☐ Read John 10v11-15**

Jesus is like a perfect shepherd. He loves His sheep (His people), and even died to rescue them!
'I am the **g** _ _ _ shepherd.' (v11)

**14 ☐ Read John 11v25-26**

Jesus is the only one who gives eternal life. If someone who believes in Jesus dies, he will be raised to life again. This is called resurrection.
'I am the **r** _ _ _ _ _ _ _ _ _ _ _ _ and the life.' (v25)

**15 ☐ Read John 14v5-6**

Jesus is the <u>only</u> way to be right with God, and to live with Him for ever in heaven.
'I am the **W** _ _ , the truth and the life. No one comes to the Father except through me.' (v6)

**16 ☐ Read John 15v1-5**

Followers of Jesus grow to live the way He wants them to—like branches on a vine grow fruit.
'I am the **v** _ _ _ , and you are the branches.' (v5)

**17 ☐ Read John 1v29**

Jesus died to take the punishment for our sin—like a perfect lamb, dying in our place.
'There is the **L** _ _ _ of God, who takes away the sin of the world.' (v29)

**18 ☐ Read Mark 10v42-45**

Even though Jesus is our King, He came to serve people, and to die as our ransom (which means paying the cost to rescue us). He is our **Servant King**!
'The Son of Man did not come to be served, but to **s** _ _ _ _ _ , and to give His life as a ransom for many.' (v45)

**19 ☐ Read Isaiah 9v6-7**

Hundreds of years before Jesus was born, Isaiah gave Him some very special titles. The first one tells us that Jesus shows us the best way to live.
'He will be called **W** _ _ _ _ _ _ _ _ _ Counsellor...' (v6)

**20 ☐ Read Isaiah 9v6-7**

Jesus is God! He is mighty and powerful.
'He will be called Wonderful Counsellor, **M** _ _ _ _ _ God...' (v6)

# Extra Readings

**21** ☐ **Read Isaiah 9v6-7**

*Jesus is everlasting! He has always existed and always will.*

'He will be called Wonderful Counsellor, Mighty God,

Everlasting **F** _ _ _ _ _ ...' (v6)

**22** ☐ **Read Isaiah 9v6-7 (again!)**

*Jesus brings us peace with God.*

'He will be called Wonderful Counsellor, Mighty God, Everlasting Father,

**P** _ _ _ _ _ of Peace.' (v6)

**23** ☐ **Read John 1v1-3**

*John starts his Gospel by telling us that Jesus is 'the Word', and that He made everything.*

'From the very **b** _ _ _ _ _ _ _ _ the Word was with God.' (v2)

**24** ☐ **Read Revelation 22v13**

*The last book in the Bible tells us that Jesus is the beginning and end of all things. Most versions say 'Alpha and Omega', which are the first and last letters in the Greek alphabet.*

'I am the Alpha and the Omega, the

**F** _ _ _ _ and the Last, the Beginning and the End.' (v13)

**25** ☐ **Read Revelation 22v16**

*In the book of Revelation, Jesus also tells us that He is like a bright star shining in the morning.*

'I am the bright Morning

**S** _ _ _ .' (v16)

**26** ☐ **Read Hebrews 13v8**

*Jesus never changes. Everything we have read about Him in these extra readings will be true for ever!*

'Jesus Christ is the same yesterday,

**t** _ _ _ _ and forever.' (v8)

## WHAT NEXT?

We hope that **Table Talk** has helped you get into a regular habit of reading the Bible with your children.

**Table Talk** comes out every three months. Each issue contains 65 full **Table Talk** outlines, plus 26 days of extra readings. By the time you've used them all, the next issue will be available.

Available from your local Christian bookshop—or call us on **0845 225 0880** to order a copy.

### COMING SOON!
### Issue Twelve of Table Talk

Issue Twelve of Table Talk explores the books of John, Daniel, Nehemiah and Revelation.

- Read about the very first Easter in **John**'s Gospel.
- Meet **Daniel**, one of the young men captured by King Nebuchadnezzar.
- Find out how the Israelites came home in **Nehemiah**.
- And explore the last book in the Bible— **Revelation**.